AUDIO ACCESS INCLUDED
Recorded Piano Accompaniments Online

PLAYBACK+
Speed • Pitch • Balance • Loop

SINGER'S JAZZ ANTHOLOGY | HIGH VOICE

pop standards

Arranged by Brent Edstrom

T0081894

To access audio visit:
www.halleonard.com/mylibrary

Enter Code
4960-7828-6658-8019

ISBN 978-1-5400-4194-4

Hal•Leonard®

Visit Hal Leonard Online at
www.halleonard.com

Contact us:
Hal Leonard
7777 West Bluemound Road
Milwaukee, WI 53213
Email: info@halleonard.com

In Europe, contact:
Hal Leonard Europe Limited
42 Wigmore Street
Marylebone, London, W1U 2RN
Email: info@halleonardeurope.com

In Australia, contact:
Hal Leonard Australia Pty. Ltd.
4 Lentara Court
Cheltenham, Victoria, 3192 Australia
Email: info@halleonard.com.au

ARRANGER'S NOTE

The vocalist's part in the *Singer's Jazz Anthology* matches the original sheet music but is *not* intended to be sung verbatim. Instead, melodic embellishments and alterations of rhythm and phrasing should be incorporated to both personalize a performance and conform to the accompaniments. In some cases, the form has been expanded to include "tags" and other endings not found in the original sheet music. In these instances, the term *ad lib.* indicates new melodic material appended to the original form.

Although the concept of personalizing rhythms and embellishing melodies might seem awkward to singers who specialize in classical music, there is a long tradition of melodic variation within the context of performance dating back to the Baroque. Not only do jazz singers personalize a given melody to fit the style of an accompaniment, they also develop a distinctive sound that helps *further* personalize their performances. Undoubtedly, the best strategy for learning how to stylize a jazz melody is to listen to recordings from the vocal jazz canon, including artists such as Nat King Cole, Ella Fitzgerald, Billie Holiday, Frank Sinatra, Sarah Vaughan, Nancy Wilson, and others.

The accompaniments in the *Singer's Jazz Anthology* can also be embellished by personalizing rhythms or dynamics, and chord labels are provided for pianists who are comfortable playing their own chord voicings. In some cases, optional, written-out improvisations are provided. These can be performed "as is," embellished, or skipped, depending on the performers' preference.

The included audio features piano recordings that can be used as a rehearsal aid or to accompany a performance. Tempi were selected to fit the character of each accompaniment, and the optional piano solos were omitted to provide a more seamless singing experience for vocalists who utilize them as backing tracks.

I hope you find many hours of enjoyment exploring the *Singer's Jazz Anthology* series!

Brent Edstrom

BLUE SUEDE SHOES

Words and Music by
CARL LEE PERKINS

Bright Swing, not too fast

Well, it's one for the mon - ey, two for the show,

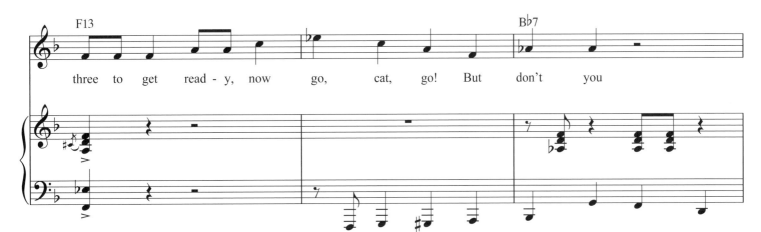

three to get read - y, now go, cat, go! But don't you

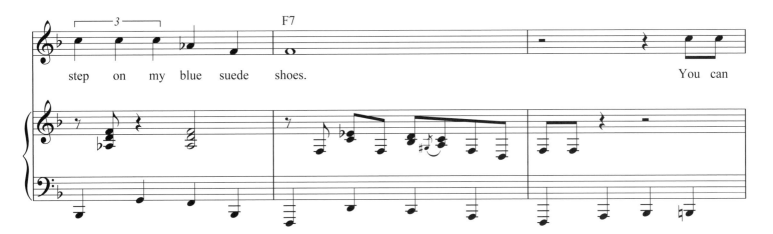

step on my blue suede shoes. You can

ALFIE
Theme from the Paramount Picture ALFIE

Words by HAL DAVID
Music by BURT BACHARACH

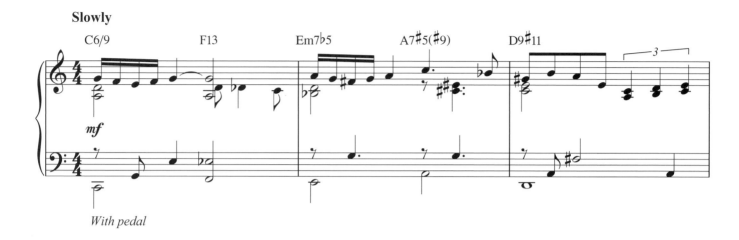

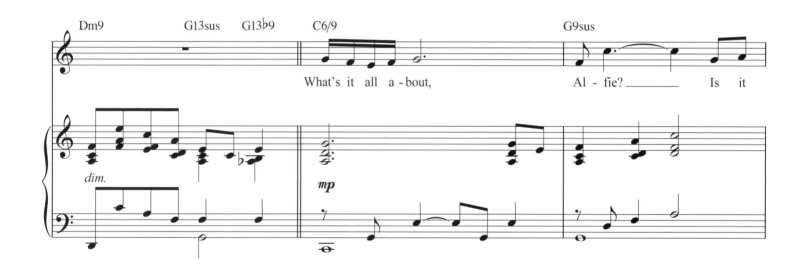

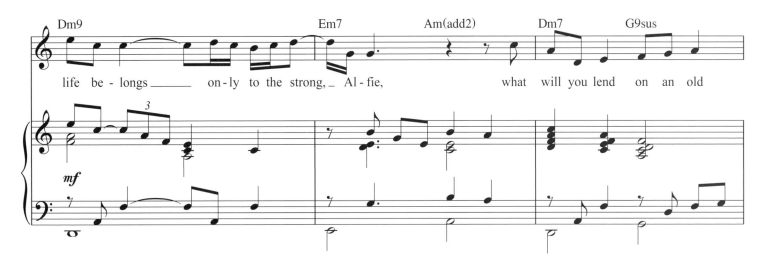

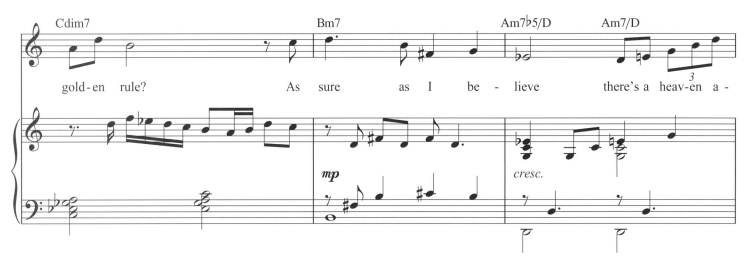

gold-en rule? As sure as I be - lieve there's a heav-en a -

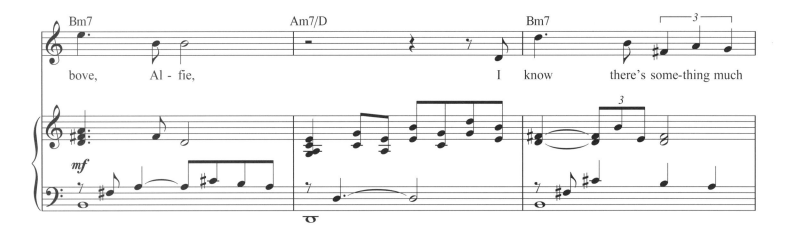

bove, Al - fie, I know there's some-thing much

more, some-thing e - ven non - be - liev - ers can be - lieve in.

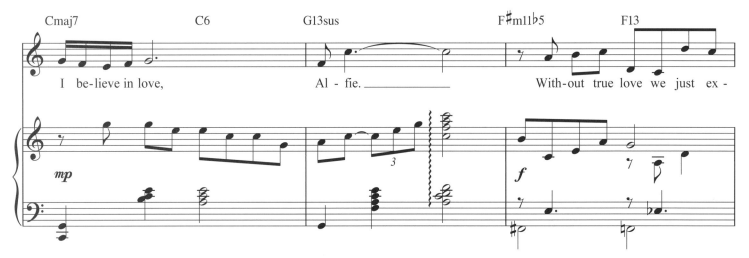

I be-lieve in love, Al - fie. With-out true love we just ex -

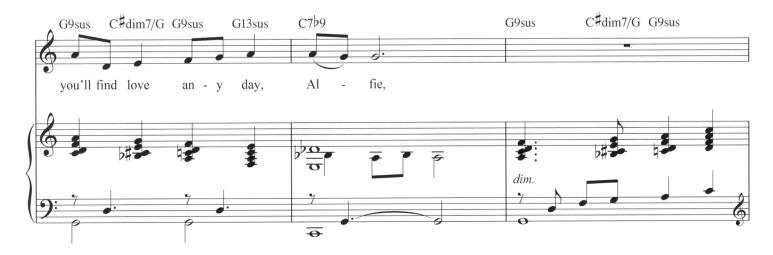

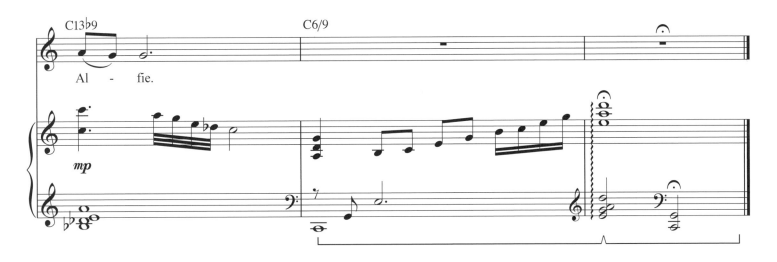

BAND OF GOLD

Words and Music by EDYTHE WAYNE
and RONALD DUNBAR

you were _____ still here _____ with me. _____ You took me _____ from the shel -

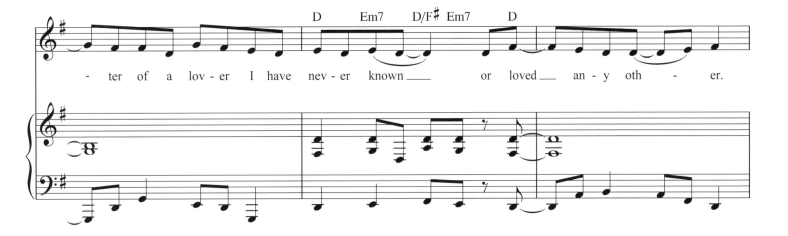

- ter of a lov - er I have nev - er known _____ or loved _____ an - y oth - er.

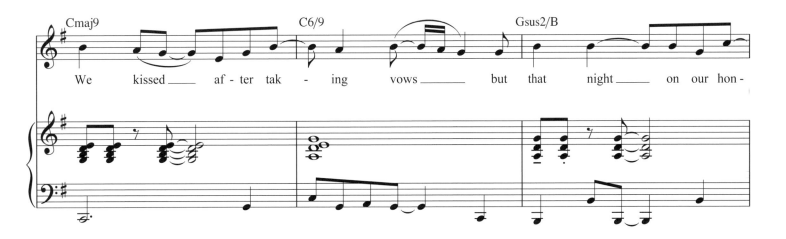

We kissed _____ af - ter tak - ing vows _____ but that night _____ on our hon -

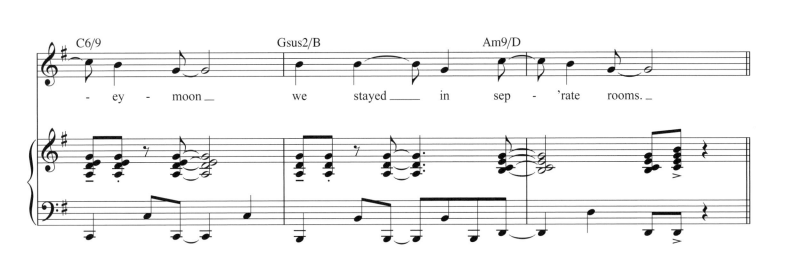

- ey - moon _____ we stayed _____ in sep - 'rate rooms. _____

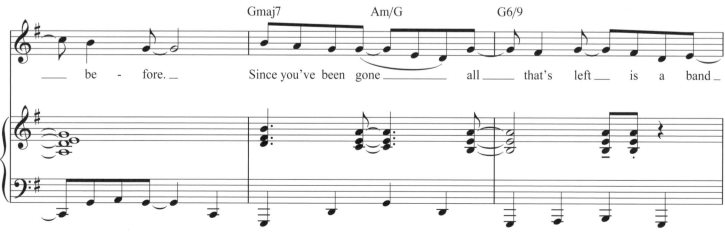

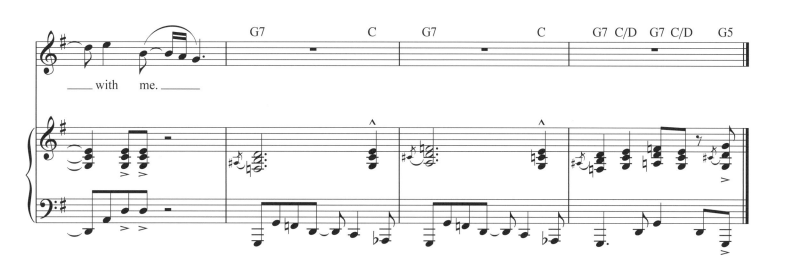

THE BEST IS YET TO COME

Music by CY COLEMAN
Lyrics by CAROLYN LEIGH

Moderate Swing

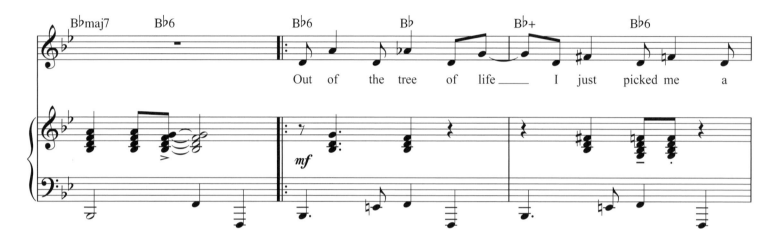

Out of the tree of life ___ I just picked me a

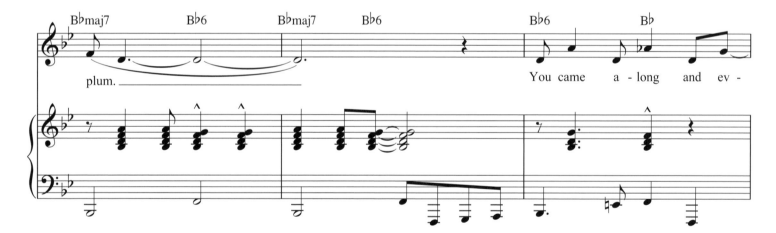

plum. ___ You came a-long and ev-

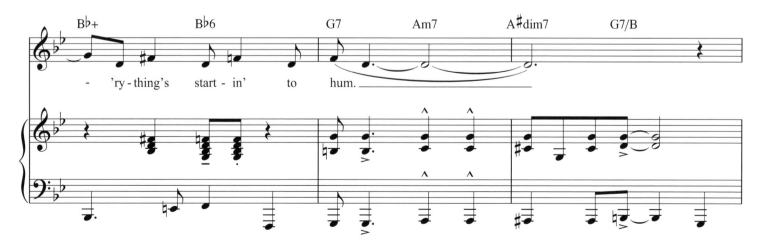

-'ry-thing's start-in' to hum. ___

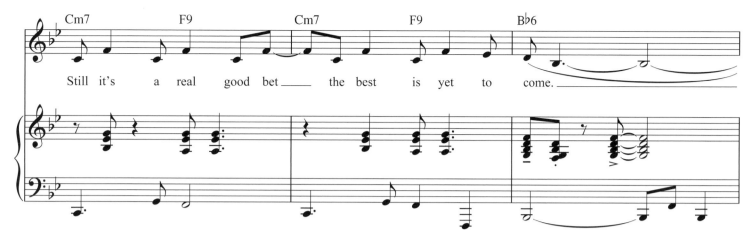

Still it's a real good bet ___ the best is yet to come. ___

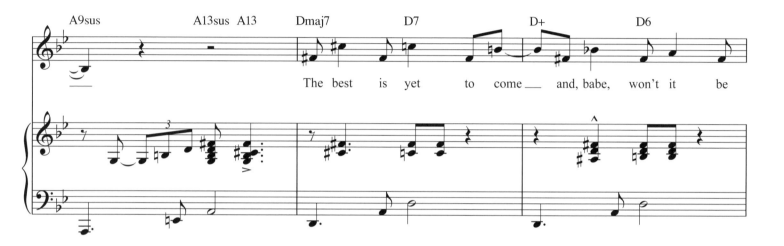

The best is yet to come ___ and, babe, won't it be

fine? ___ You think you've seen the sun ___

___ but you ain't seen it shine.

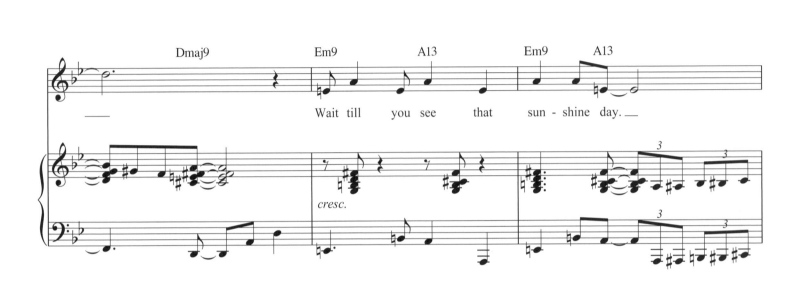

18

dry. _____ Wait till your charms are ripe _

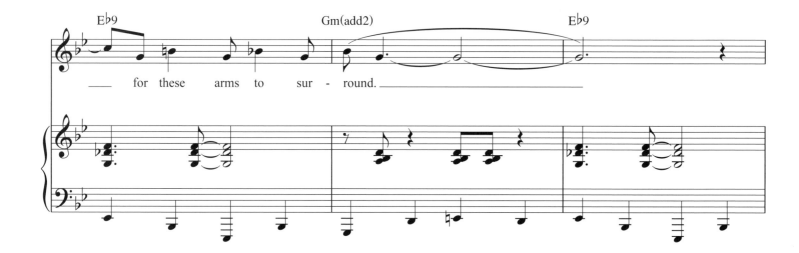

_ for these arms to sur - round. _____

You think you've flown be - fore, __ but you ain't left the ground. ____

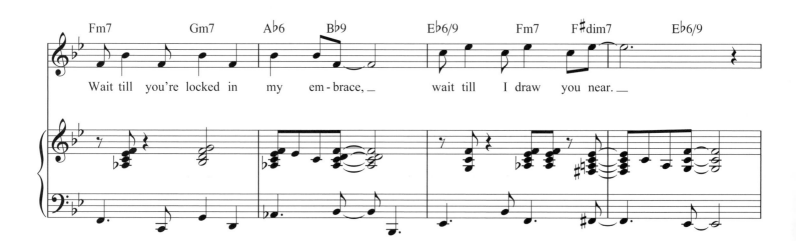

Wait till you're locked in my em - brace, _ wait till I draw you near. _

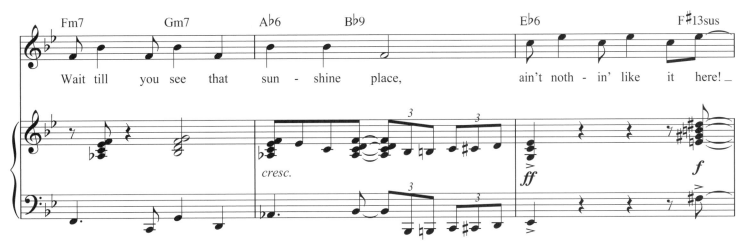

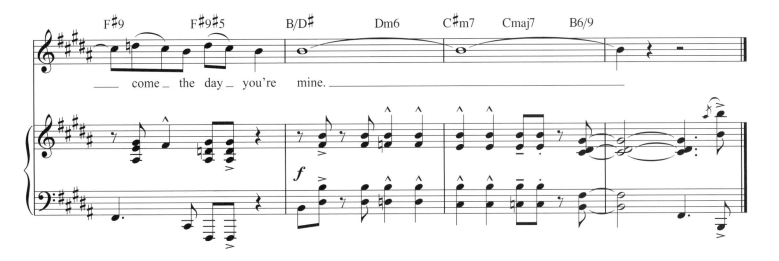

BLACKBIRD

Words and Music by JOHN LENNON
and PAUL McCARTNEY

Slowly and smoothly

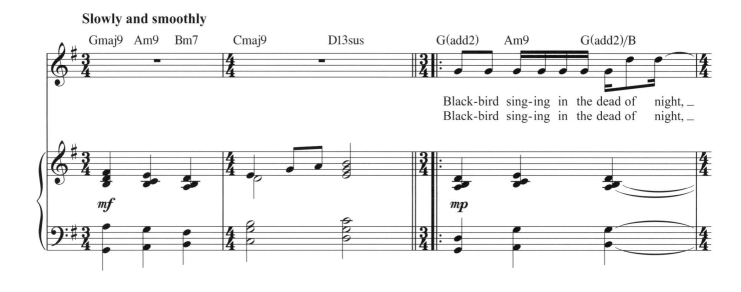

Black-bird sing-ing in the dead of night, _
Black-bird sing-ing in the dead of night, _

take these bro-ken wings _ and learn to fly; _
take these sunk-en eyes _ and learn to see; _

all your life ___ you were on-ly wait-ing for this mo-ment to a-
all your life ___ you were on-ly wait-ing for this mo-ment to be

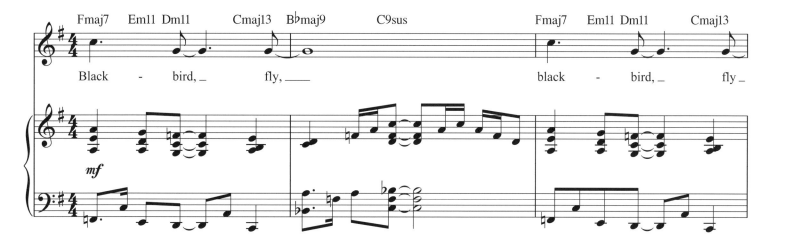

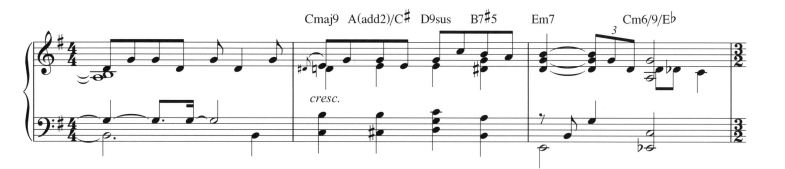

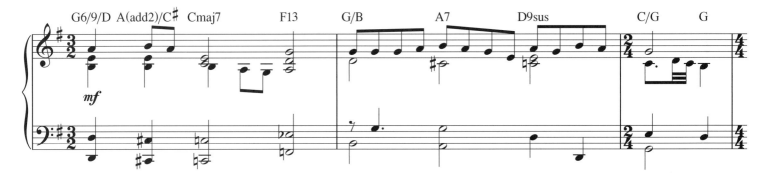

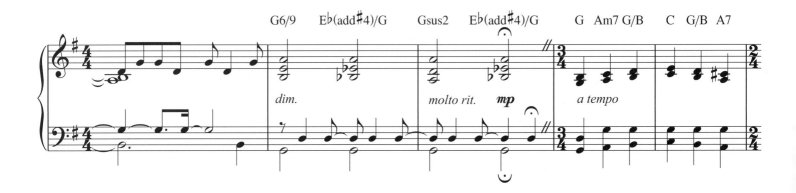

BRIDGE OVER TROUBLED WATER

Words and Music by
PAUL SIMON

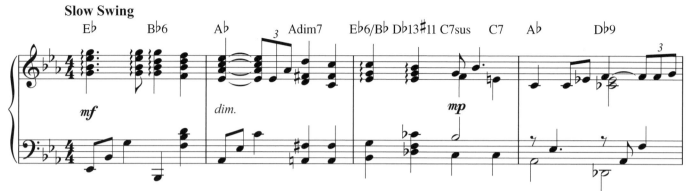

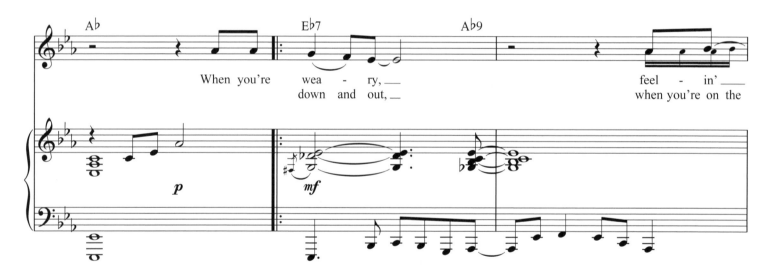

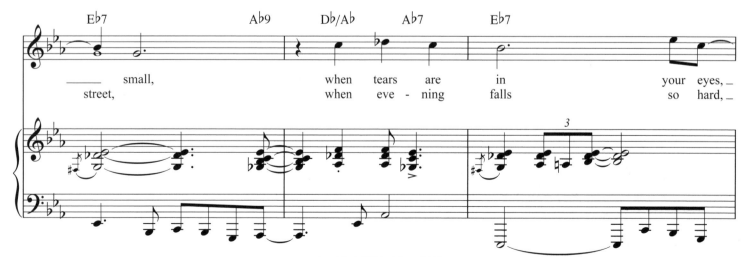

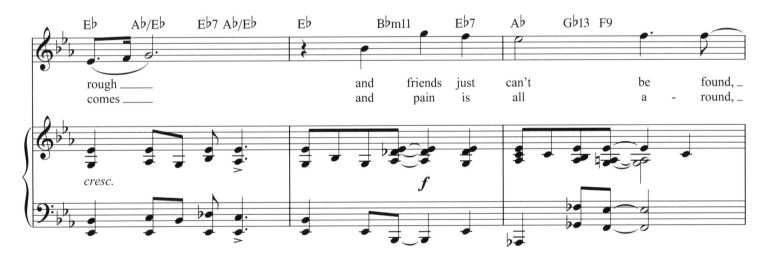
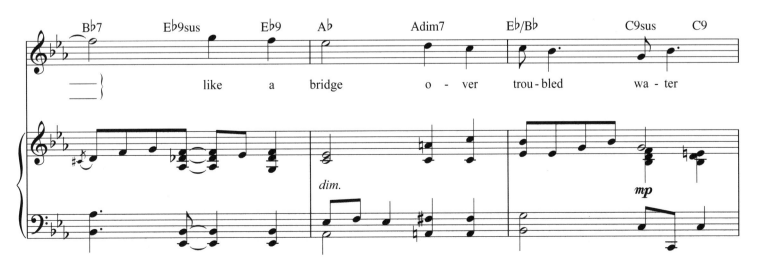

I will lay me down. Like a bridge o - ver

trou-bled wa - ter I will lay me down.

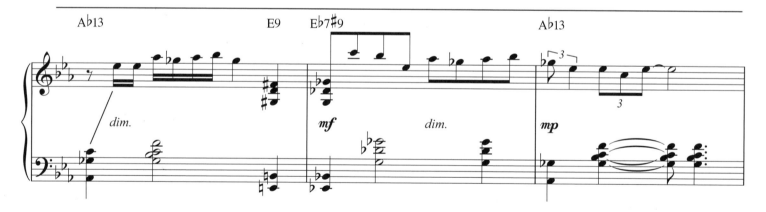

When you're trou-bled wa-ter

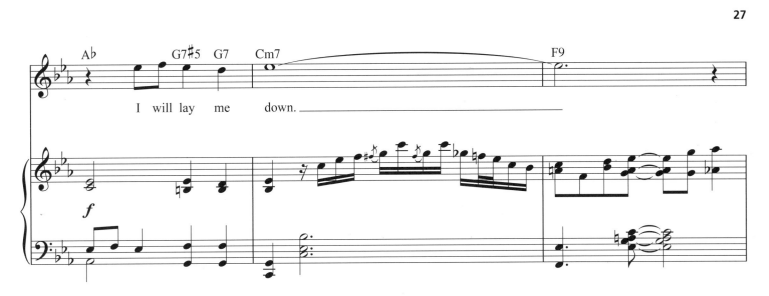

I will lay me down. _____

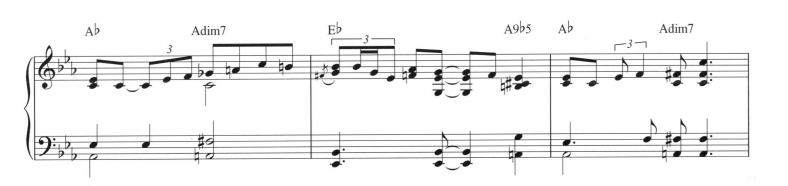

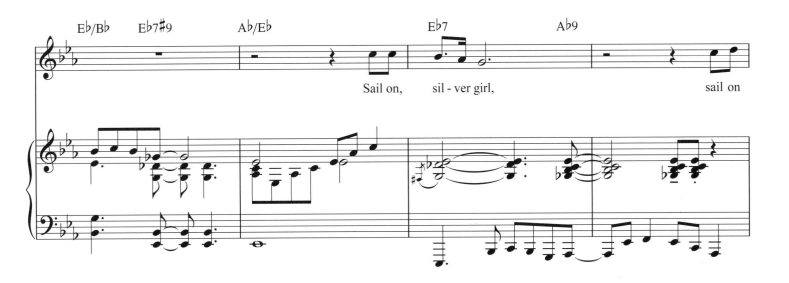

Sail on, sil - ver girl, sail on

DREAM A LITTLE DREAM OF ME

Words by GUS KAHN
Music by WILBUR SCHWANDT and FABIAN ANDREE

Stars shin-ing bright a-bove you,

night breez-es seem to whis-per, "I love you," birds sing-ing in the

syc-a-more tree, dream a lit-tle dream of me.

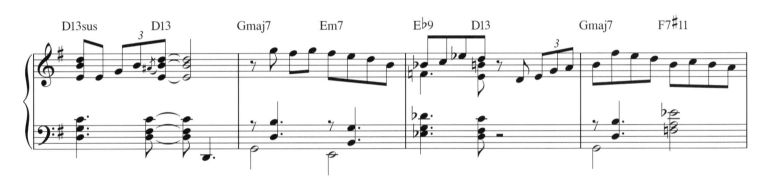

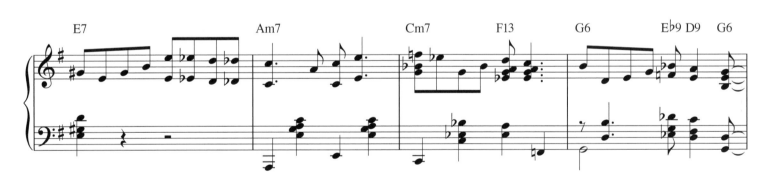

EVERY BREATH YOU TAKE

Music and Lyrics by
STING

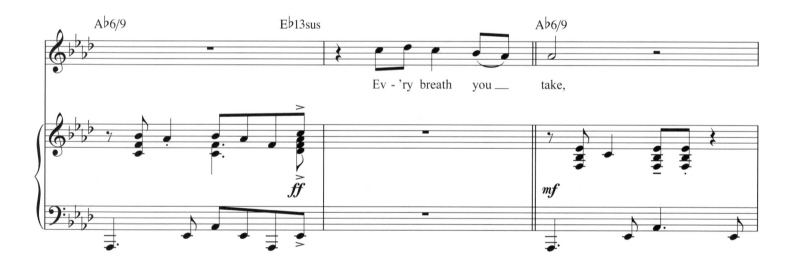

Ev - 'ry breath you ___ take,

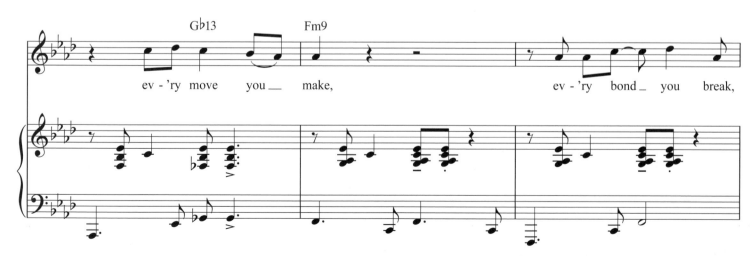

ev - 'ry move you ___ make,   ev - 'ry bond ___ you break,

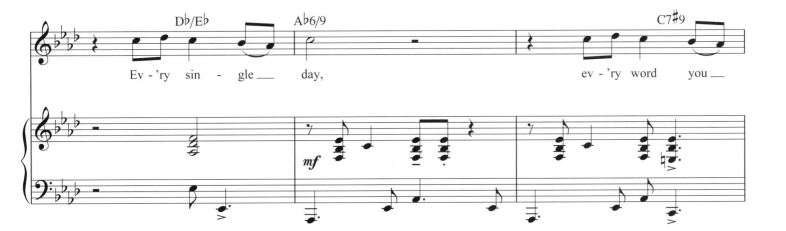

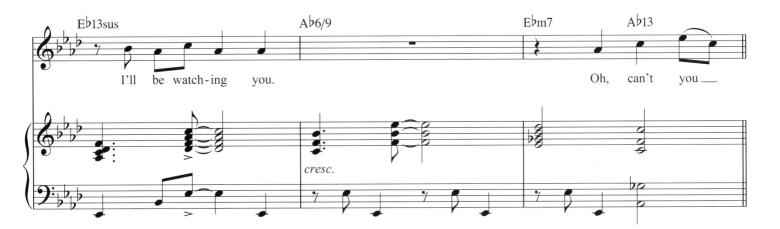

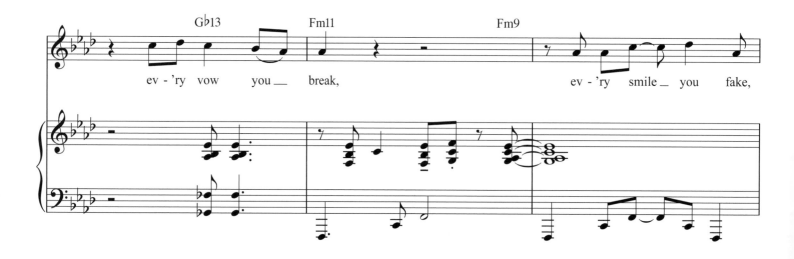

To Coda ⊕

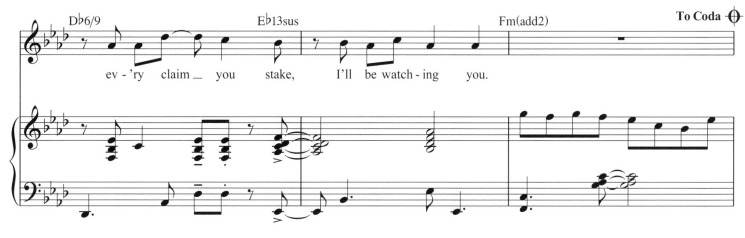

ev - 'ry claim ___ you stake, I'll be watch - ing you.

Since you've gone, ___ I been lost ___ with - out ___ a trace,

I dream at night I can on - ly see ___ your face. I look a - round, but it's

you I can't ___ re - place. I feel so cold and I long for your ___ em - brace.

I keep cry - ing, ba - by, ba - by, please. _____

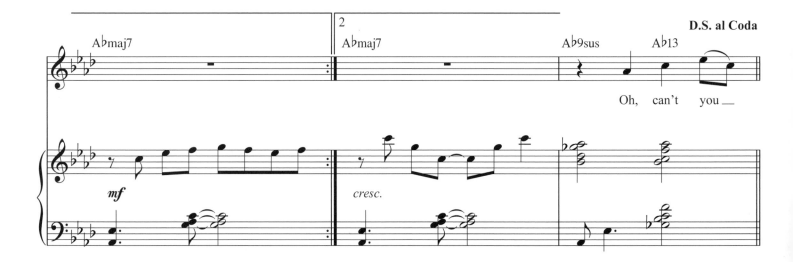

Oh, can't you __

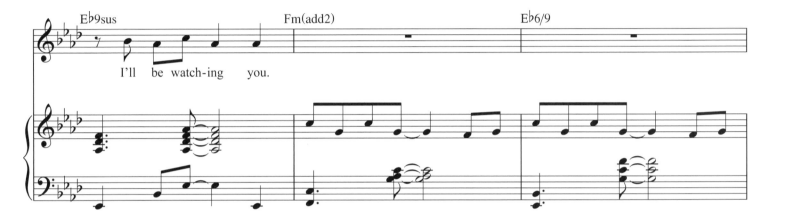

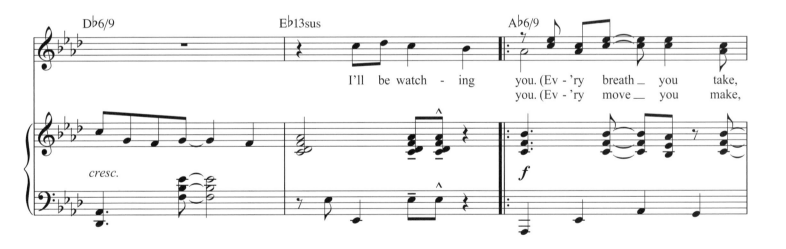

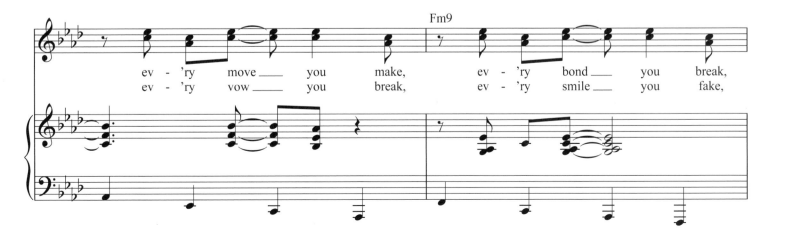

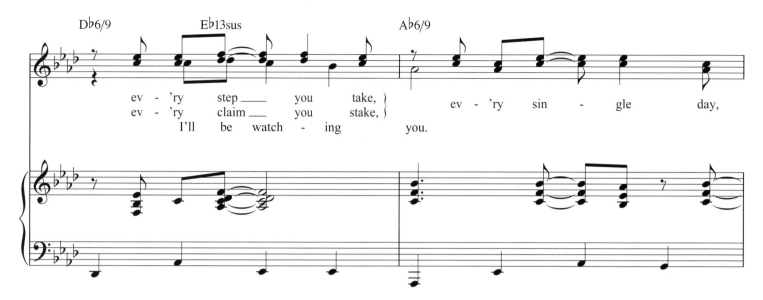

ev - 'ry step___ you take,   ev - 'ry sin - gle day,
ev - 'ry claim___ you stake, }
I'll be watch - ing you.

ev - 'ry word_ you say,   ev - 'ry game_ you play,   ev - 'ry night_ you stay.)
I'll be watch - ing

Straight 8ths

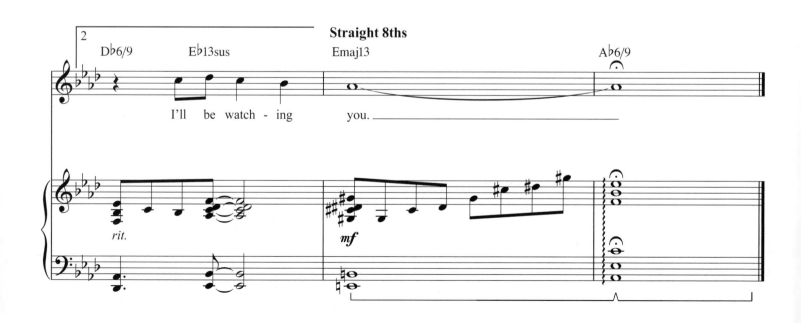

I'll be watch - ing you.___

rit.   *mf*

THE LOOK OF LOVE
from CASINO ROYALE

Words and Music by HAL DAVID
and BURT BACHARACH

Medium Swing

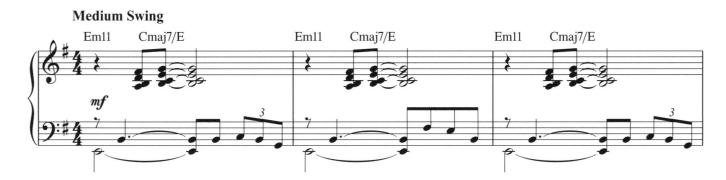

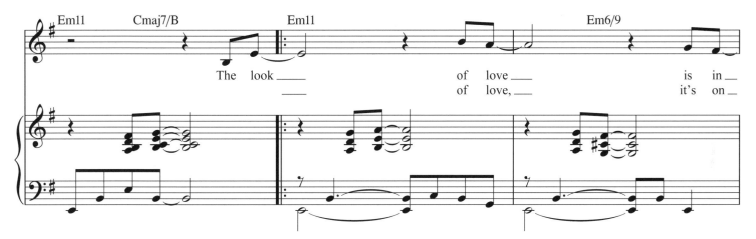

The look _____ of love _____ is in _____
_____ of love, _____ it's on _____

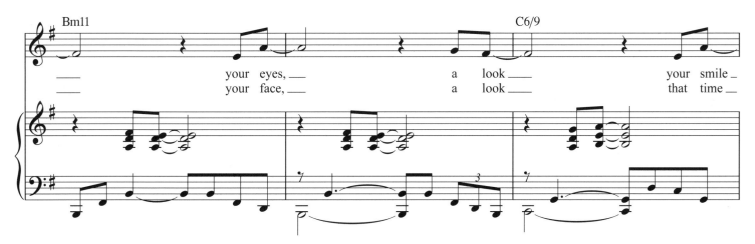

_____ your eyes, _____ a look _____ your smile _____
_____ your face, _____ a look _____ that time _____

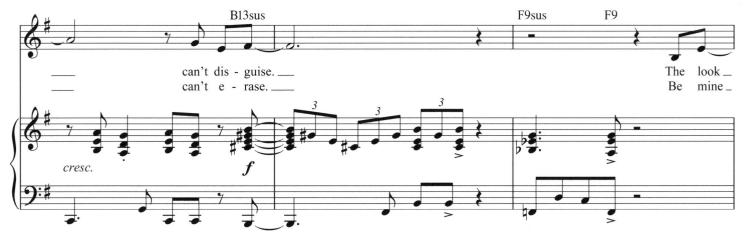

_____ can't dis - guise. _____ The look _____
_____ can't e - rase. _____ Be mine _____

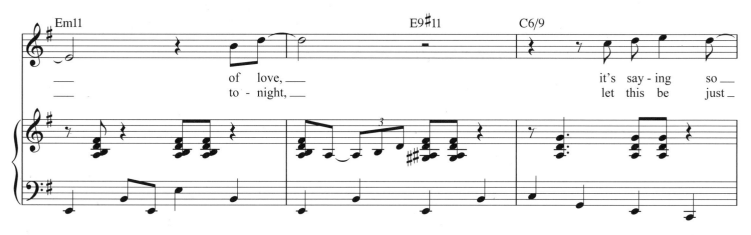

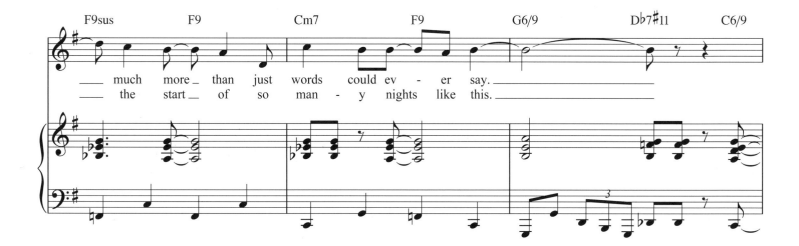

FIRE AND RAIN

Words and Music by
JAMES TAYLOR

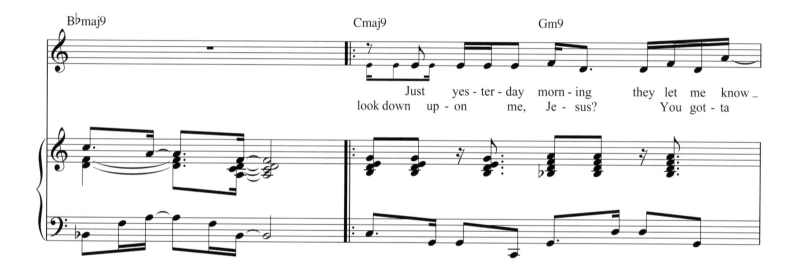

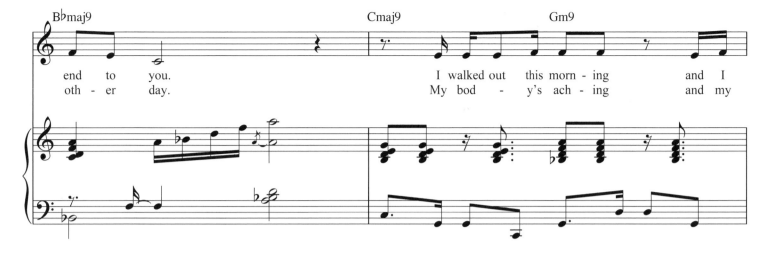

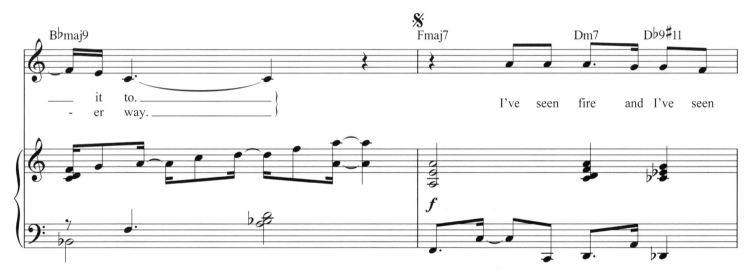

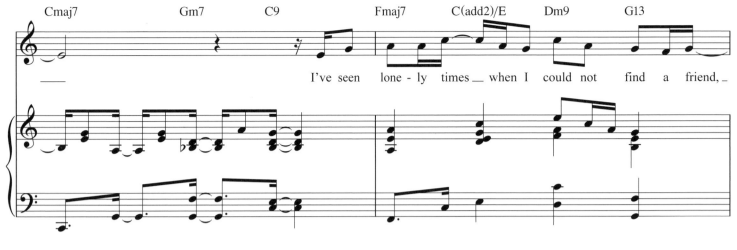

I've seen lone-ly times — when I could not find a friend, —

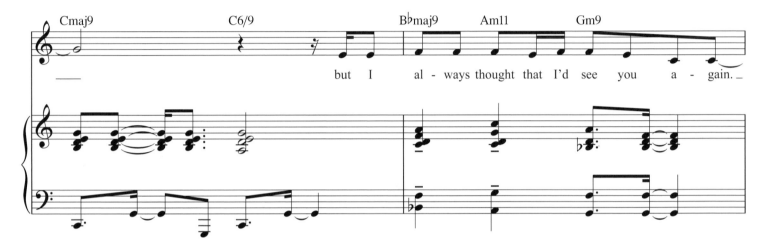

but I al-ways thought that I'd see you a - gain. —

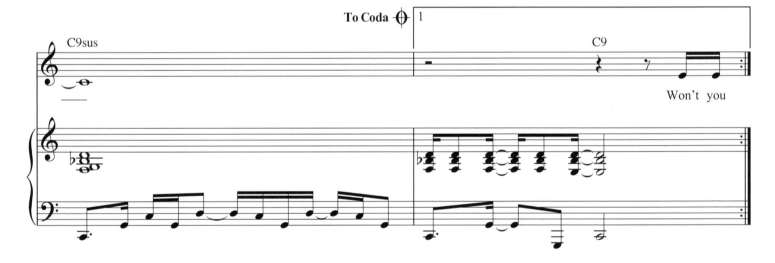

To Coda

Won't you

Now I'm walk-ing my mind to an eas-y time, my

GOODBYE YELLOW BRICK ROAD

Words and Music by ELTON JOHN
and BERNIE TAUPIN

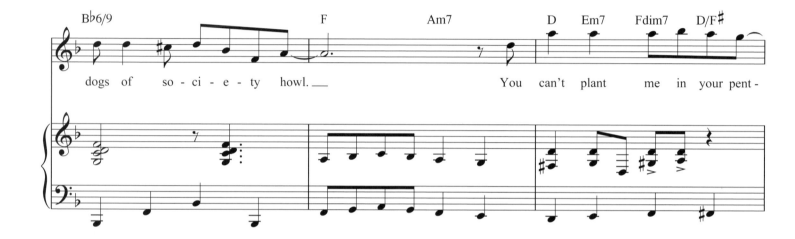

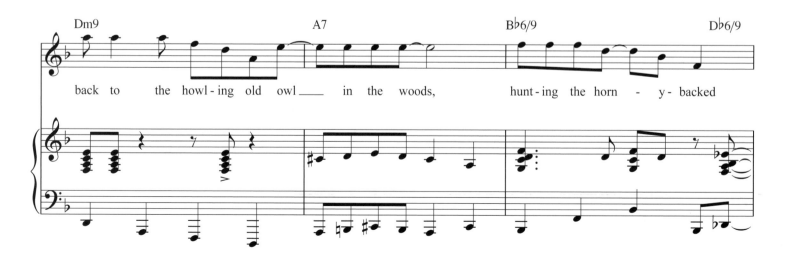

I CAN'T STOP LOVING YOU

Words and Music by
DON GIBSON

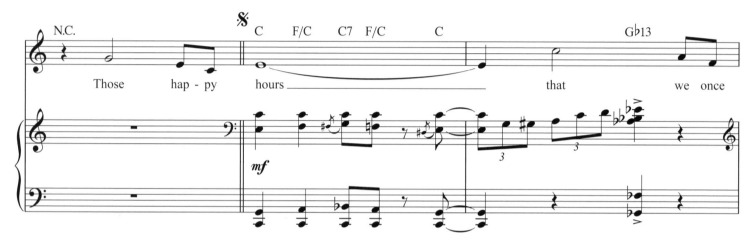

Those hap-py hours _____ that we once

knew, _____ though long a-go,

_____ still make me blue. _____ They say that

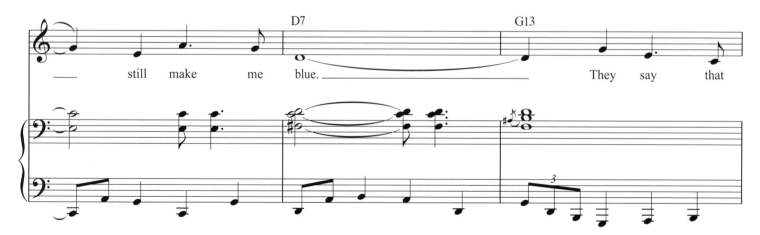

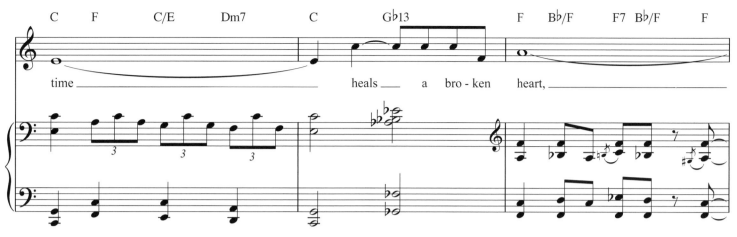

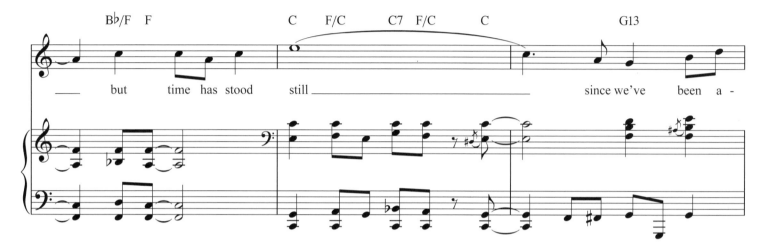

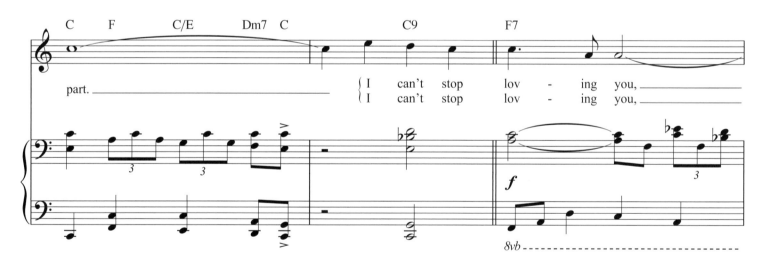

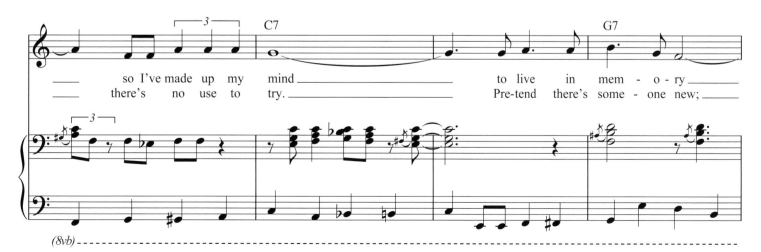

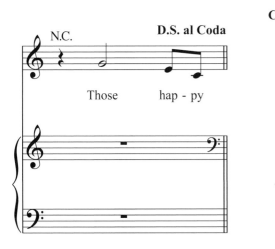

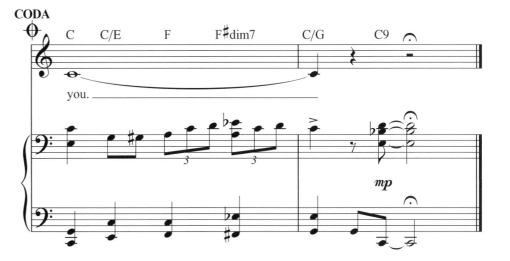

I HEARD IT THROUGH THE GRAPEVINE

Words and Music by NORMAN J. WHITFIELD
and BARRETT STRONG

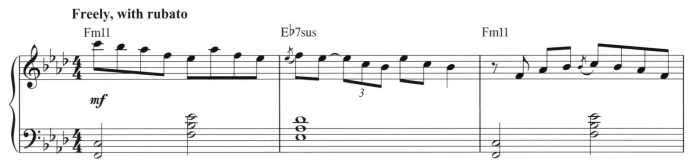

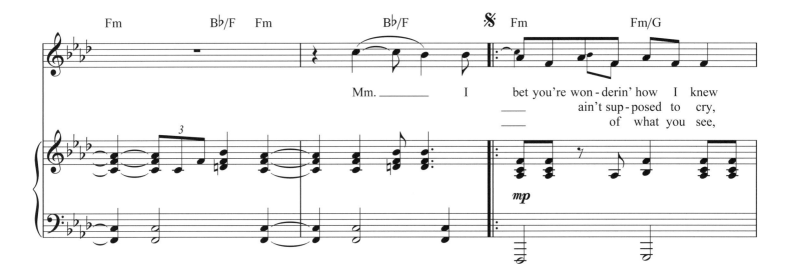

Mm. _____ I bet you're won-derin' how I knew
_____ ain't sup-posed to cry,
_____ of what you see,

'bout your plans _____ to make me blue, _____ with some oth-er guy _____
but these tears _____ I can't hold in-side. _____ Los-in' you _____
son, and none _____ of what you hear. _____ But I can't help _____

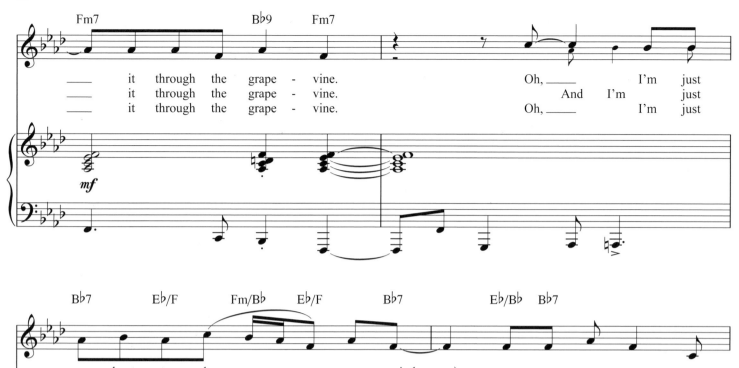

it through the grape - vine. Oh, _____ I'm just
it through the grape - vine. And I'm just
it through the grape - vine. Oh, _____ I'm just

a - bout to lose _____ my mind. _____ } Hon - ey, hon - ey, oh
a - bout to lose _____ my mind. _____ } Hon - ey, hon - ey, oh
a - bout to lose _____ my mind. _____ } Hon - ey, hon - ey, (I

yeah.
heard it through the grape - vine, not much long - er would you be mine, ba -

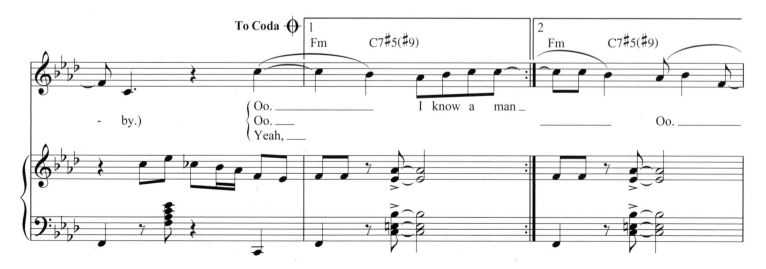

- by.)
Oo. _____   I know a man _____
Oo. _____   _____ Oo.
Yeah, _____

Peo-ple say be-lieve half

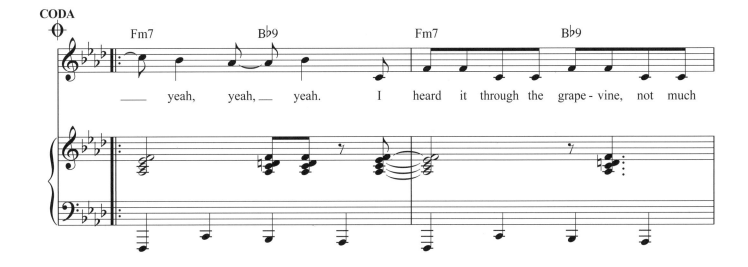

___ yeah, yeah, ___ yeah. I heard it through the grape - vine, not much

long - er would you be mine, ba — by. Yeah, __ - by.

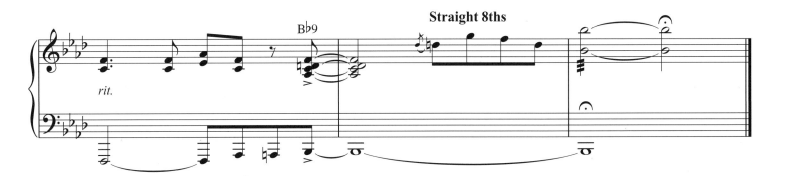

ISN'T SHE LOVELY

Words and Music by
STEVIE WONDER

Is - n't she love - ly,
pret - ty,
love - ly,

is - n't she won - der - ful? _____ Is - n't she
tru - ly the an - gels' best? _____ Boy, I'm so
life and love are the same. _____ Life is A -

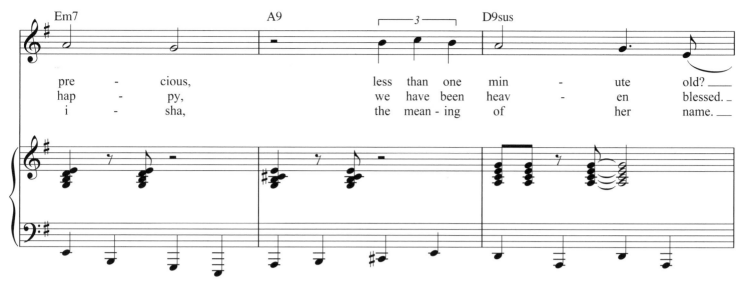

pre - cious,
hap - py,
i - sha,

less than one min - ute old? ___
we have been heav - en blessed. ___
the mean - ing of her name. ___

___ I nev - er thought ___ through love we'd be ___ mak - ing
___ I can't be - lieve ___ what God has done, ___ through us
___ Lon - die, it could ___ have not been done ___ with - out

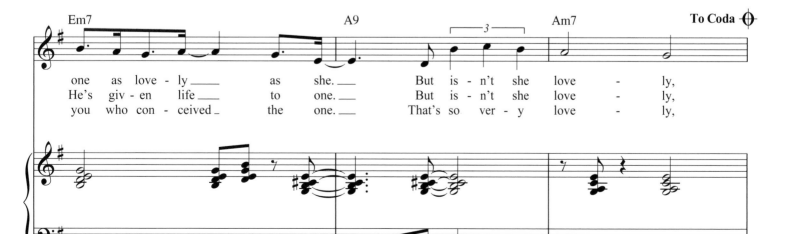

one as love - ly ___ as she. ___ But is - n't she love - ly,
He's giv - en life ___ to one. ___ But is - n't she love - ly,
you who con - ceived ___ the one. ___ That's so ver - y love - ly,

To Coda

62

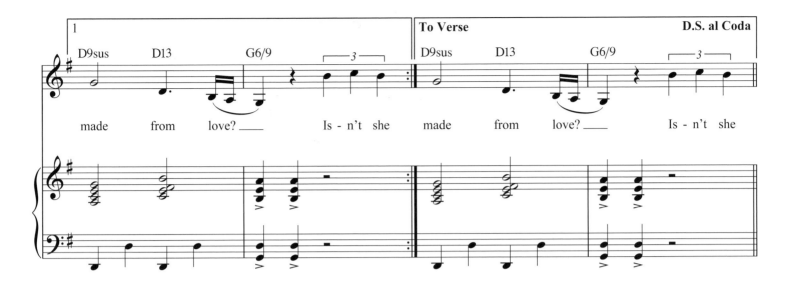

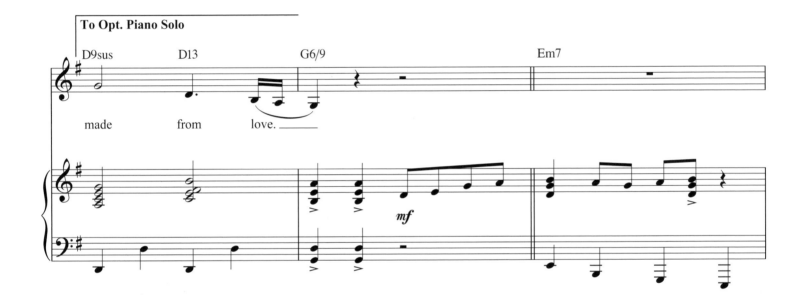

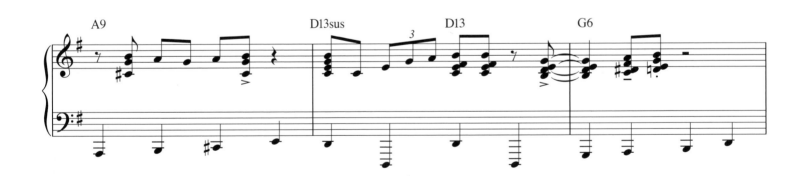

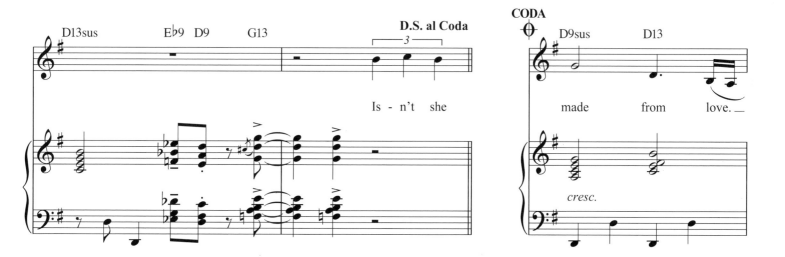

Is - n't she

made   from   love. __

MEDITATION
(Meditação)

Music by ANTONIO CARLOS JOBIM
Original Words by NEWTON MENDONÇA
English Words by NORMAN GIMBEL

Relaxed Bossa Nova

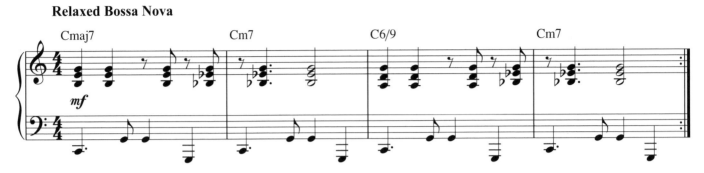

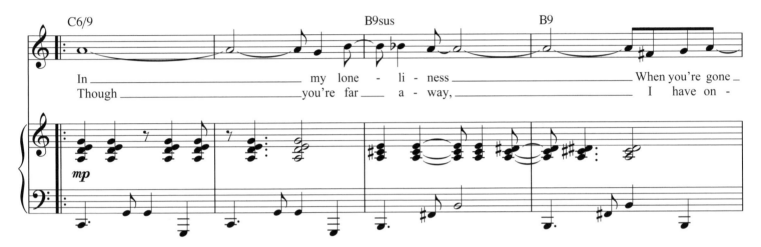

In _____ my lone - li - ness _____ When you're gone _____
Though _____ you're far a - way, _____ I have on -

____ and I'm all ____ by my - self ____ and I ____ need your ____ ca - ress, _____
- ly to close ____ my eyes ____ and you are back ____ to stay. _____

____ I _____ just think ____ of you _____
____ I _____ just close ____ my eyes _____

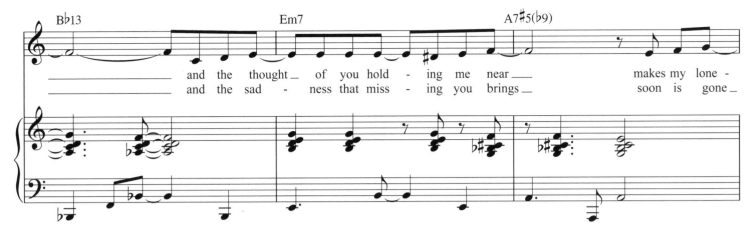

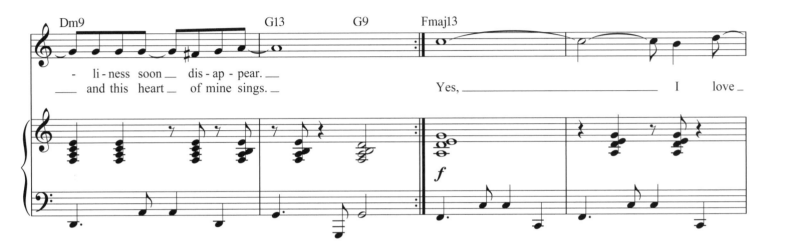

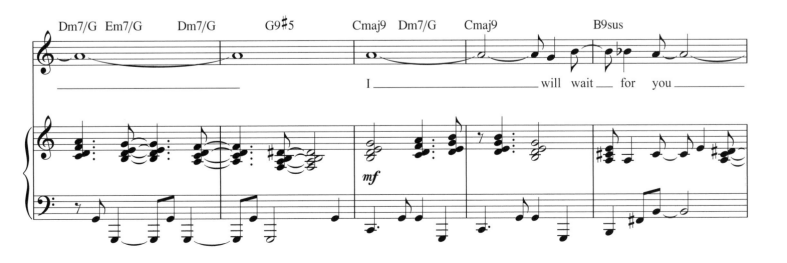

'til the sun ___ falls from out ___ of the sky ___ for what ___ else can ___ I do? ___

___ I ___ will wait ___ for you, ___

___ med - i - tat - ing how sweet ___ life will be ___ when you come ___ back to me.

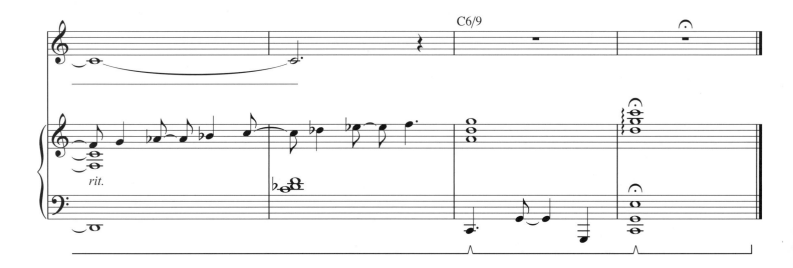

ROLLING IN THE DEEP

Words and Music by ADELE ADKINS
and PAUL EPWORTH

Funky groove

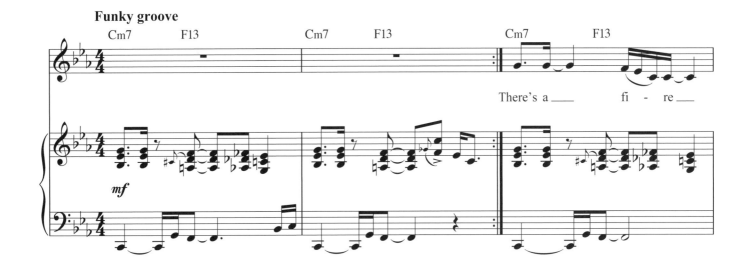

There's a ___ fi - re

start-ing in my ___ heart, reach-ing ___ a fe-ver pitch and bring-ing me out the dark. ___

Fi - nal - ly ___ I can see you crys-tal clear, go a-head ___ and sell me out and

I'll lay your shit bare. See how _ I'll _ leave _ with ev-er-y piece of you,
Ba - by, _ I _ have _ no sto - ry to be told

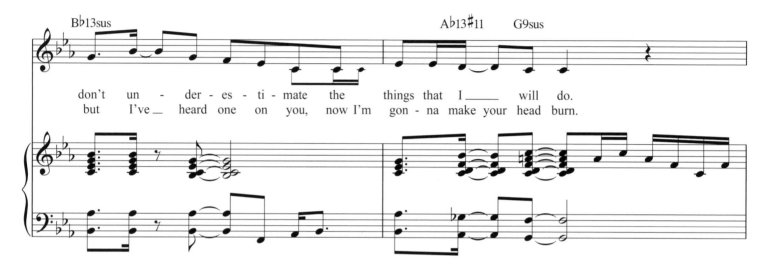

don't un - der - es - ti - mate the things that I _ will do.
but I've _ heard one on you, now I'm gon - na make your head burn.

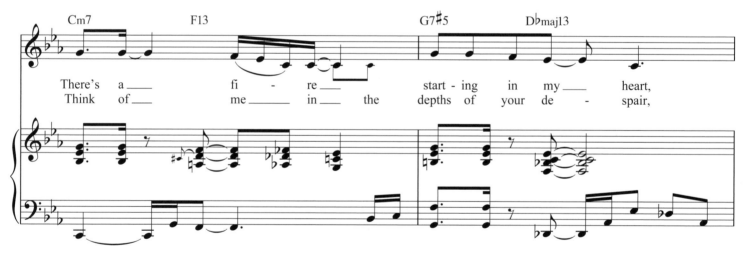

There's a _ fi - re _ start - ing in my _ heart,
Think of _ me _ in _ the depths of your de - spair,

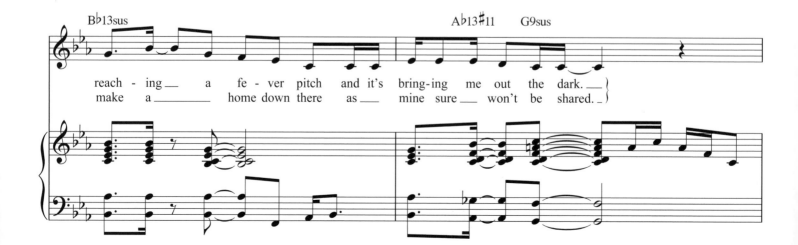

reach - ing _ a fe - ver pitch and it's bring-ing me out the dark. _
make a _ home down there as _ mine sure _ won't be shared. _

70

SINCERELY

Words and Music by ALAN FREED
and HARVEY FUQUA

Moderate Swing

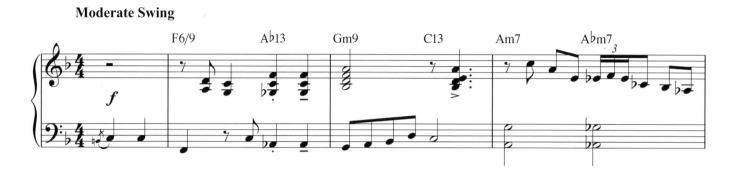

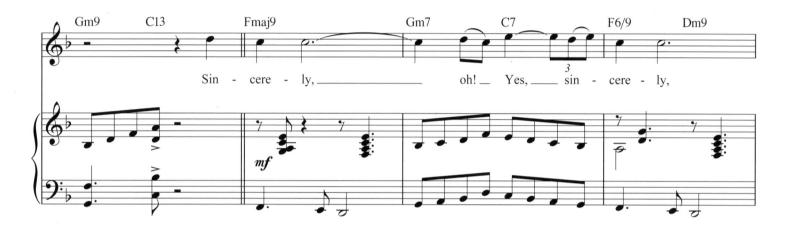

Sin - cere - ly, _____ oh! Yes, ____ sin - cere - ly,

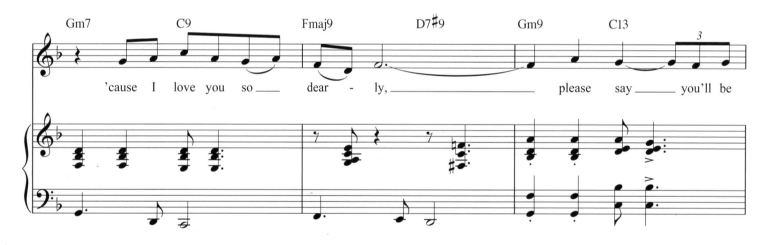

'cause I love you so ___ dear - ly, _____ please say ___ you'll be

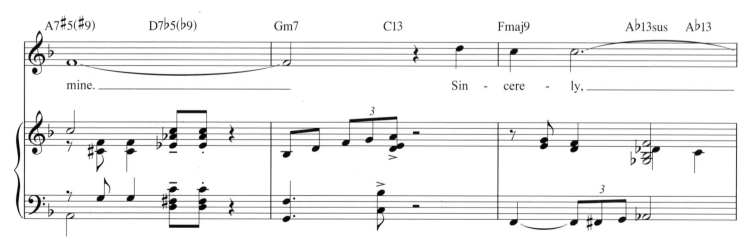

mine. _____ Sin - cere - ly, _____

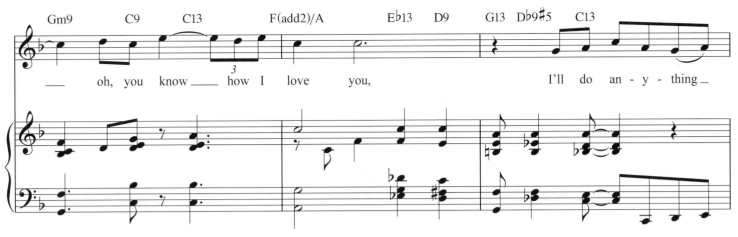

oh, you know ___ how I love you, I'll do an-y-thing ___

for ___ you, _____ please say ___ you'll be mine. _____

Oh, Lord, won't you tell ___ me why ___ I

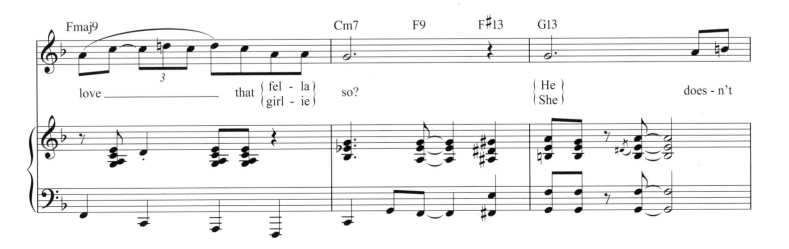

love _____ that { fel - la } so? { He } does - n't
{ girl - ie } { She }

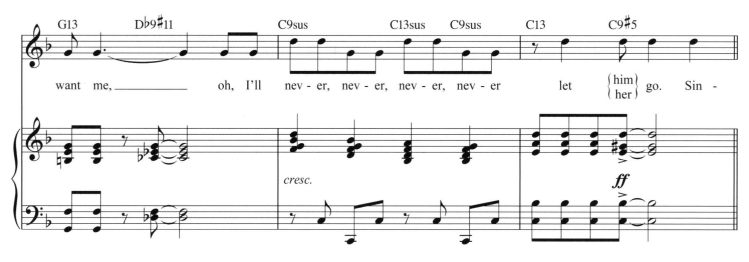

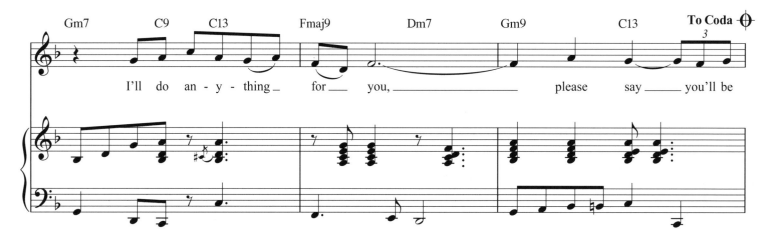

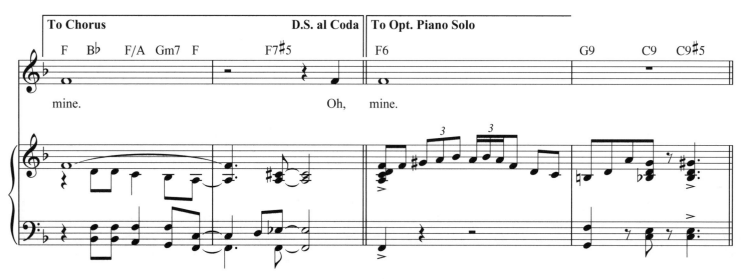

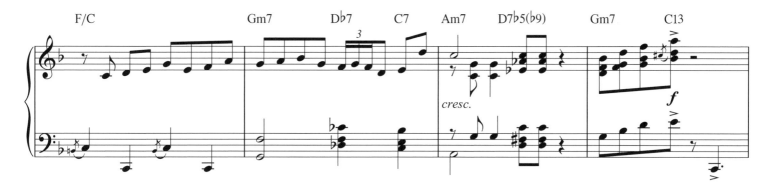

D.S. al Coda

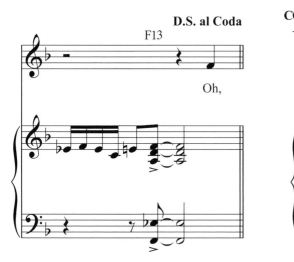

Oh,

CODA

mine.

(Sittin' On)
THE DOCK OF THE BAY

Words and Music by STEVE CROPPER
and OTIS REDDING

still re-mains the same. I can't do what ten peo-ple tell me to do,

so I guess I'll re-main the same.

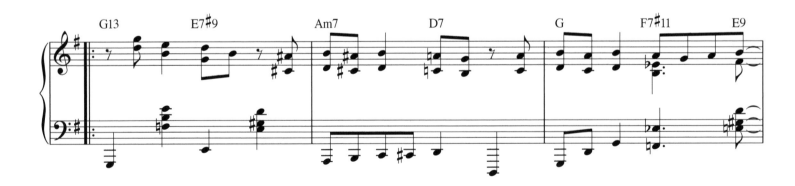

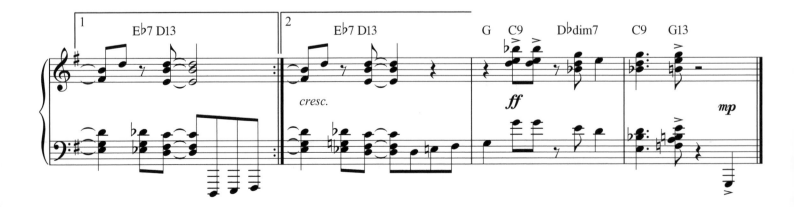

UNCHAIN MY HEART

Words and Music by BOBBY SHARP
and TEDDY POWELL

Moderately slow Swing

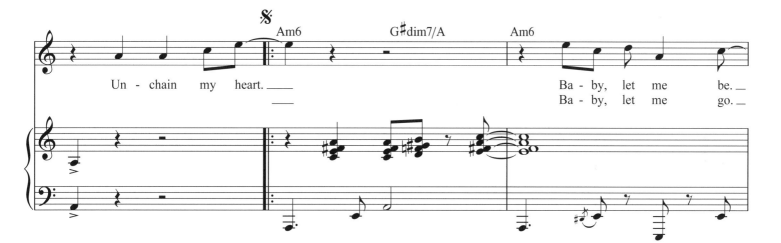

Un - chain my heart. _____
_____

Ba - by, let me be. _____
Ba - by, let me go. _____

Un - chain my heart, _____
Un - chain my heart, _____

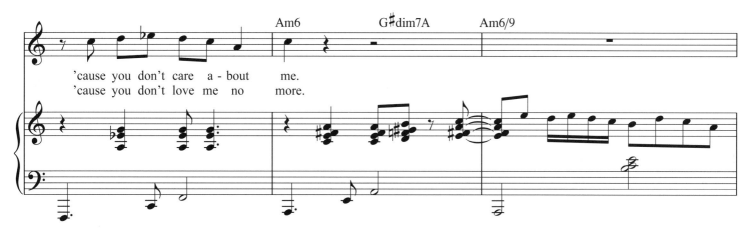

'cause you don't care a - bout me.
'cause you don't love me no more.

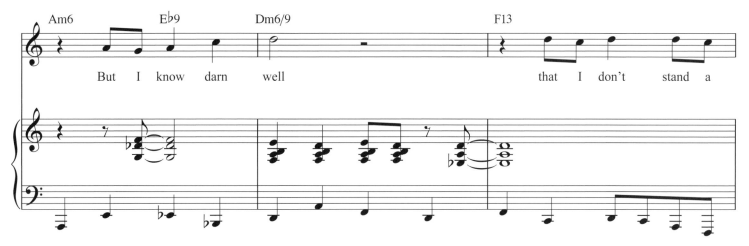

But I know darn well that I don't stand a

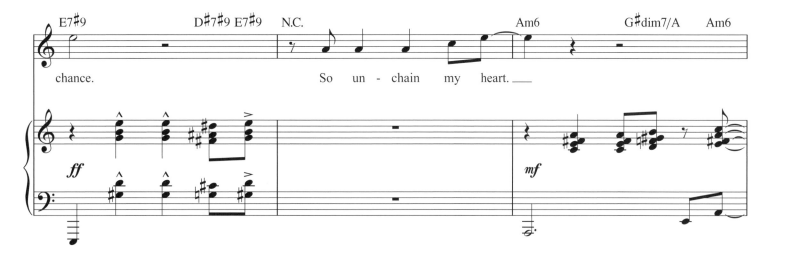

chance. So un-chain my heart. ___

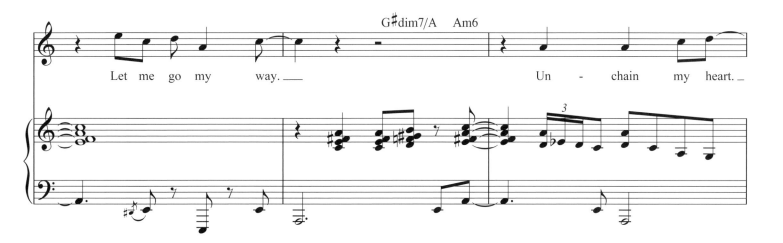

Let me go my way. ___ Un-chain my heart. ___

You wor - ry me night and day. _____

Why lead me through a life of mis - er - y, _____

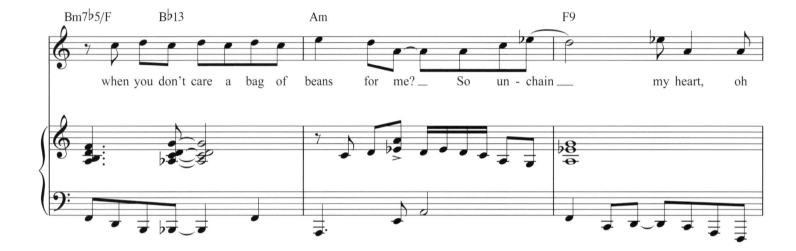

when you don't care a bag of beans for me? _ So un - chain ___ my heart, oh

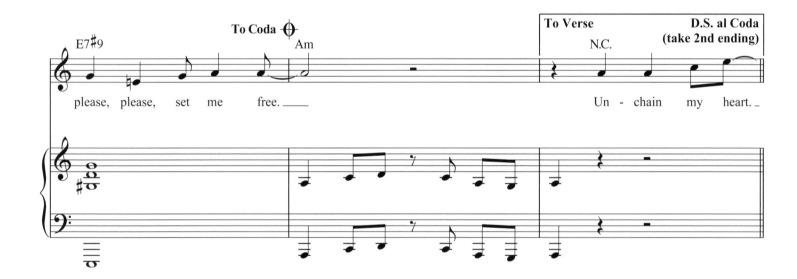

To Coda

please, please, set me free. ____

To Verse

**D.S. al Coda
(take 2nd ending)**

Un - chain my heart. _

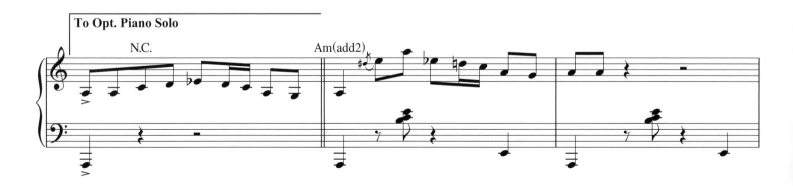

To Opt. Piano Solo

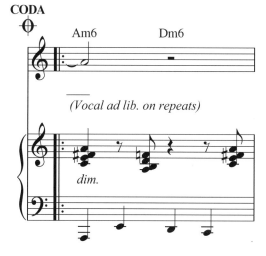

Un - chain my heart. ___

(Vocal ad lib. on repeats)

dim.

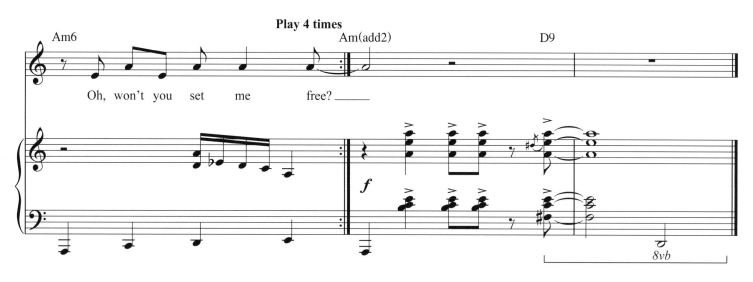

Play 4 times

Oh, won't you set me free? _____

f

8vb

SWEET DREAMS
(Are Made of This)

Words and Music by ANNIE LENNOX
and DAVID STEWART

Moderately slow Swing

Sweet dreams are made ___ of this. ___

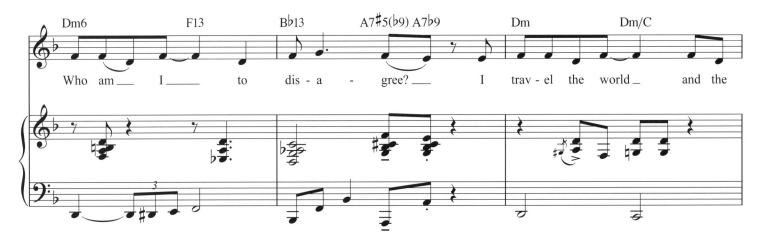

Who am ___ I ___ to dis - a - gree? ___ I trav - el the world ___ and the

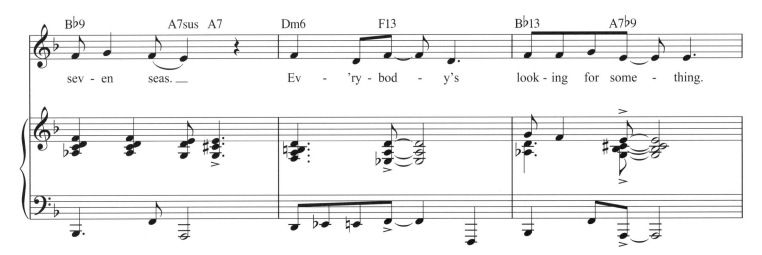

sev - en seas. ___ Ev - 'ry - bod - y's look - ing for some - thing.

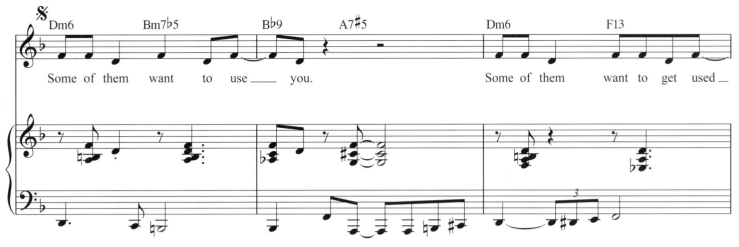

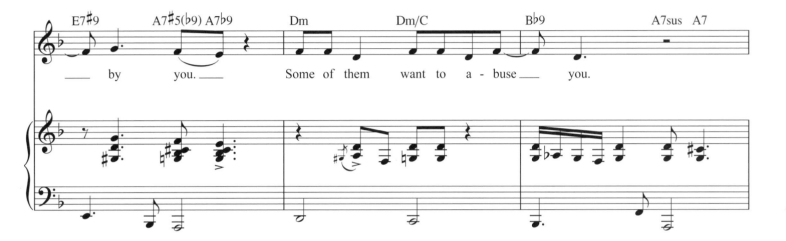

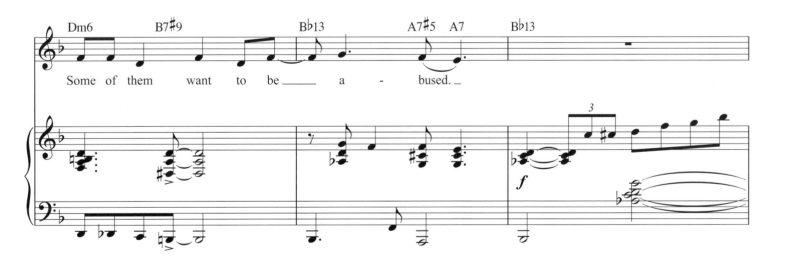

Keep your head up.

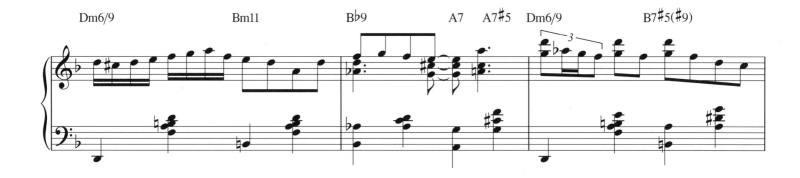

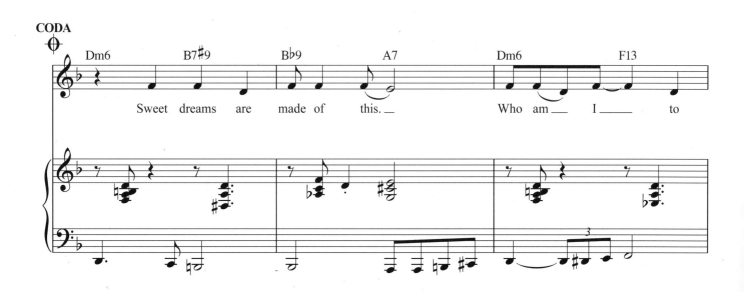

Sweet dreams are made of this. __ Who am __ I ____ to

dis - a - gree? ___ I trav - el the world ___ and the sev - en seas. ___

Ev - 'ry - bod - y's look - ing for some - thing.

THREE TIMES A LADY

Words and Music by
LIONEL RICHIE

Jazz Waltz

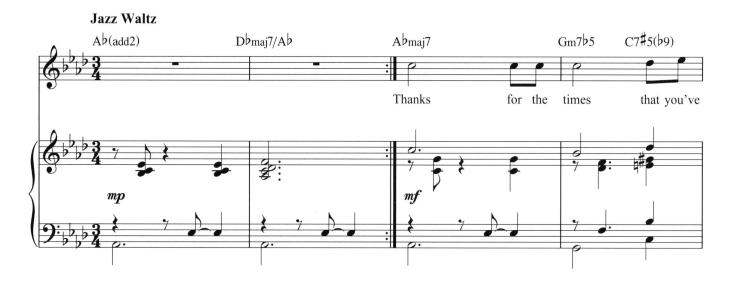

Thanks for the times that you've

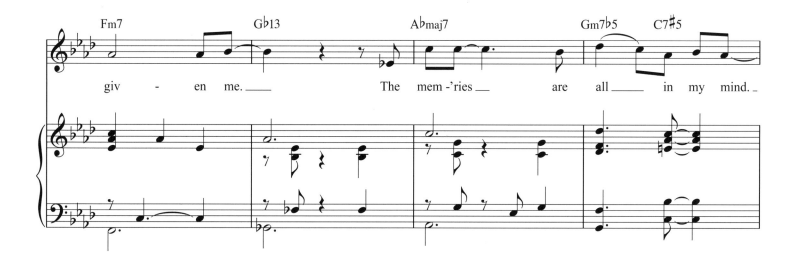

giv-en me.___ The mem-'ries ___ are all ___ in my mind. ___

___ And now that we've come to the

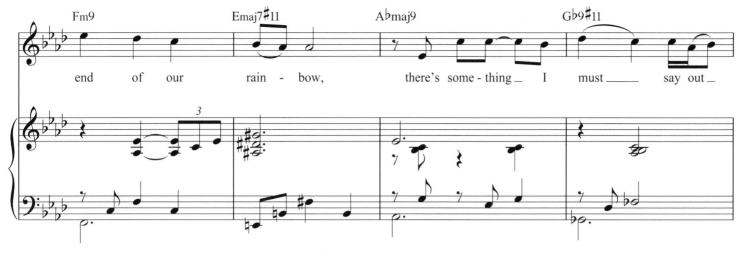

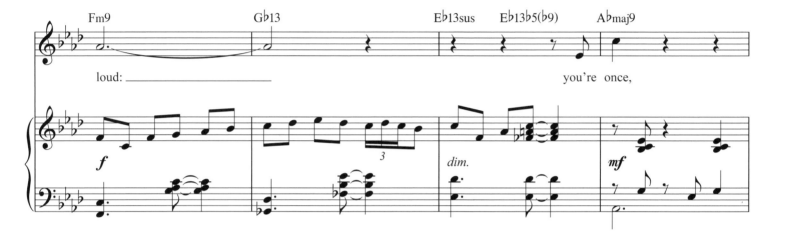

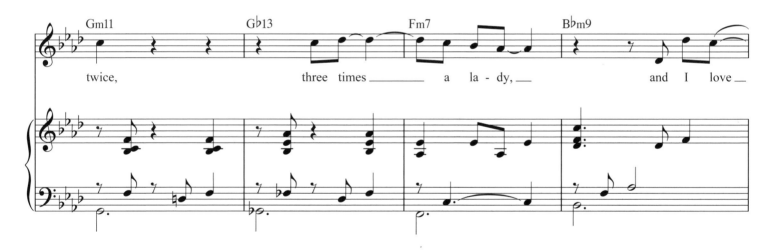

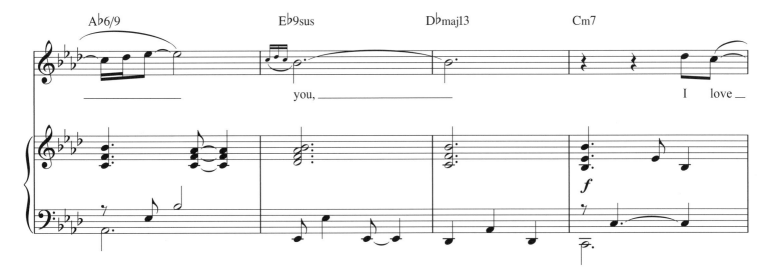

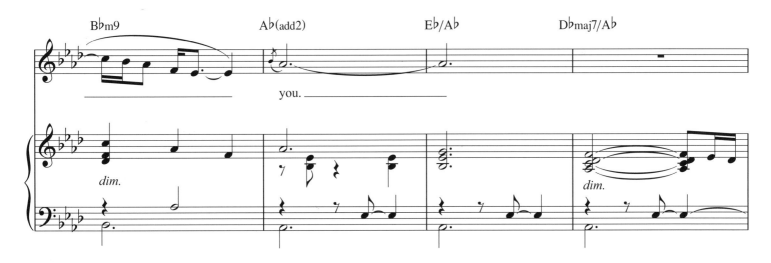

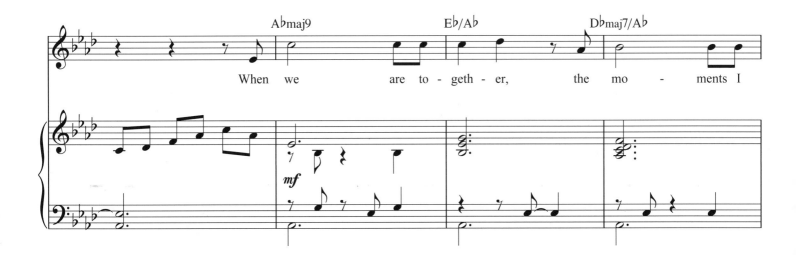

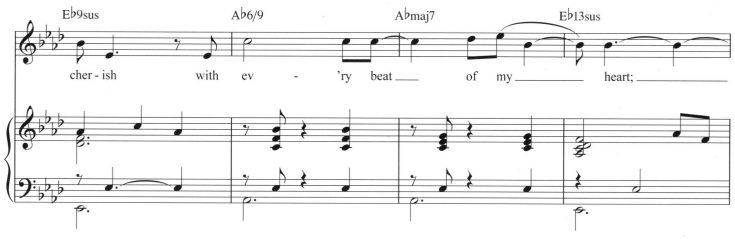

cher - ish with ev - 'ry beat ___ of my ___ heart; ___

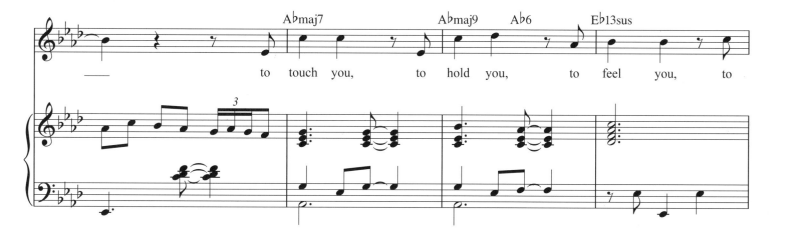

___ to touch you, to hold you, to feel you, to

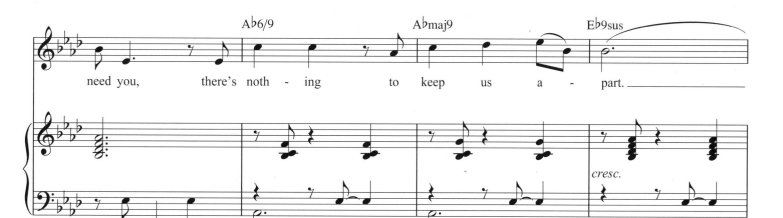

need you, there's noth - ing to keep us a - part. ___

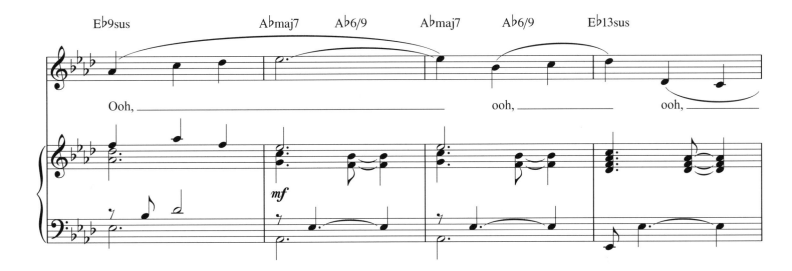

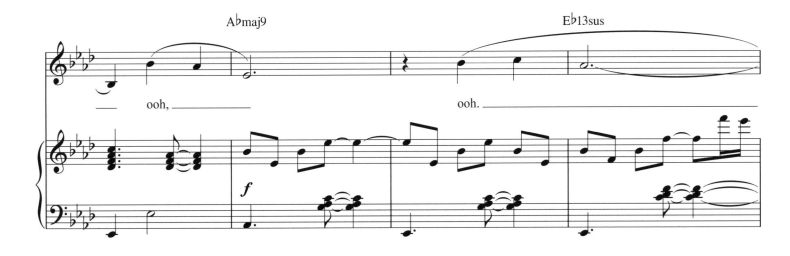

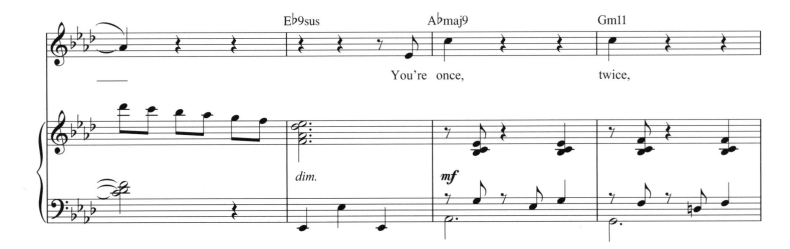

three times _____ a la - dy, _____ and I love _____

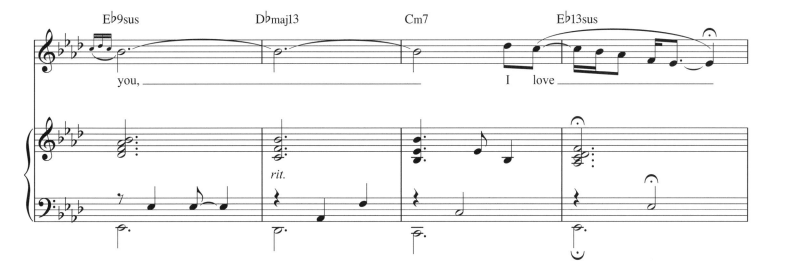

you, _____ I love _____

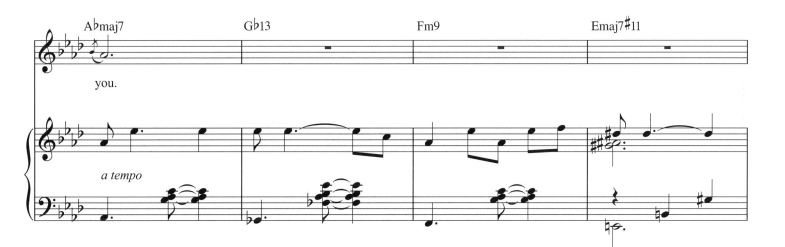

you.

Straight 8ths

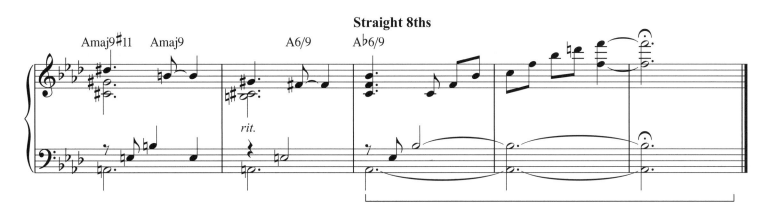

WHAT THE WORLD NEEDS NOW IS LOVE

Lyric by HAL DAVID
Music by BURT BACHARACH

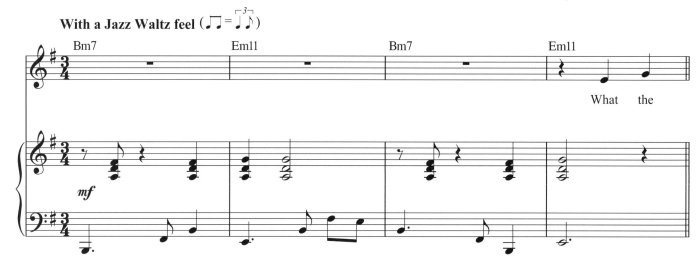

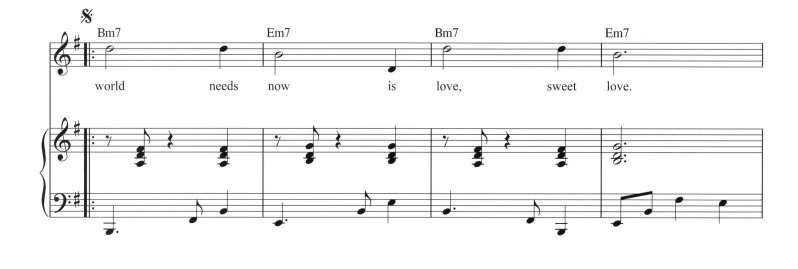

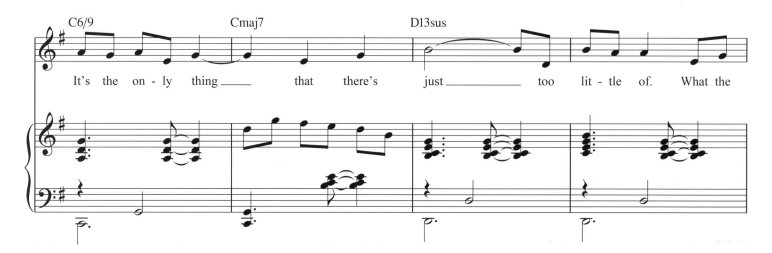

world needs now is love, sweet love. No, not just for some,

To Coda ⊕

___ but for ev - 'ry - one. ___
{ Lord, we don't
{ Lord, we don't

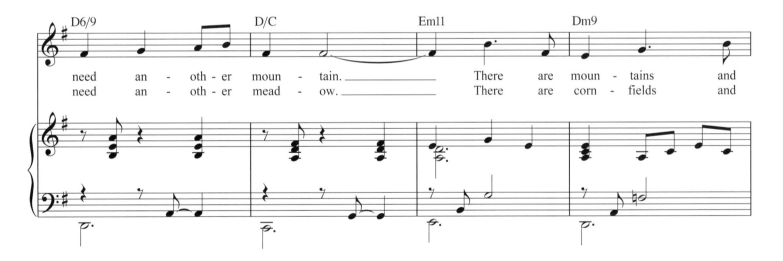

need an - oth - er moun - tain. ___ There are moun - tains and
need an - oth - er mead - ow. ___ There are corn - fields and

hill - sides e - nough to climb. ___ There are o - ceans and
wheat - fields e - nough to grow. ___ There are sun - beams and

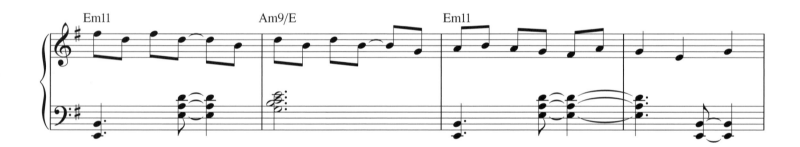

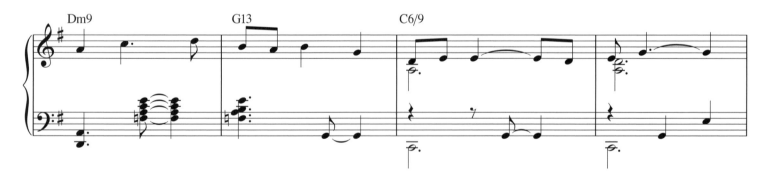

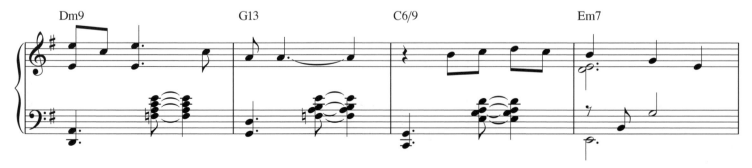

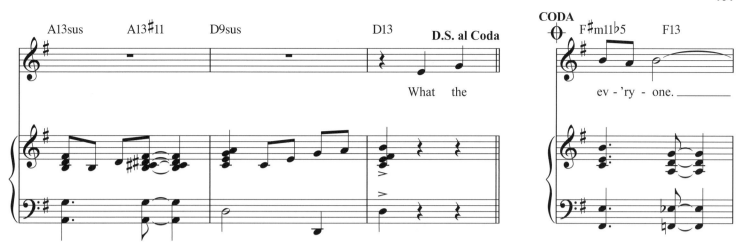

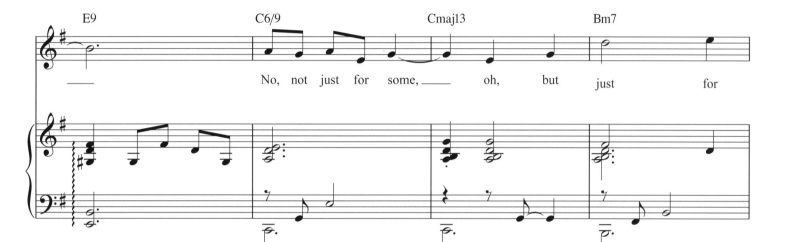

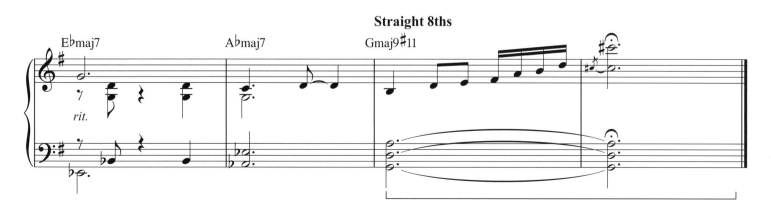

WITCHCRAFT

Music by CY COLEMAN
Lyrics by CAROLYN LEIGH

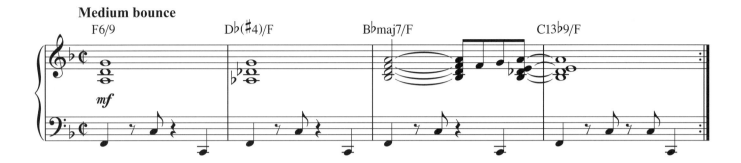

Shades of old Lu-cre-tia Bor-gia! There's a dev-il in

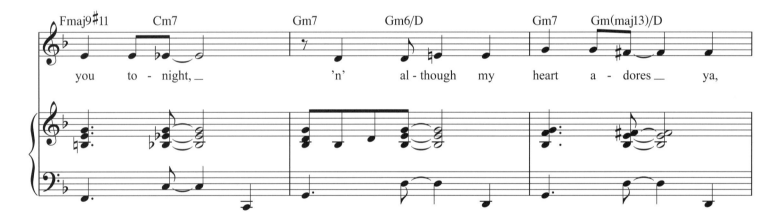

you to-night, __ 'n' al-though my heart a-dores __ ya,

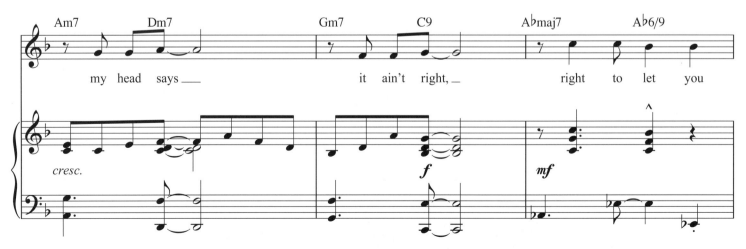

my head says __ it ain't right, __ right to let you

make ad - vanc - es, oh no! _____ Un - der nor - mal

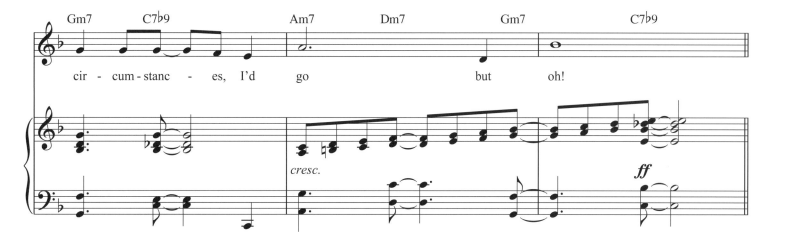

cir - cum - stanc - es, I'd go but oh!

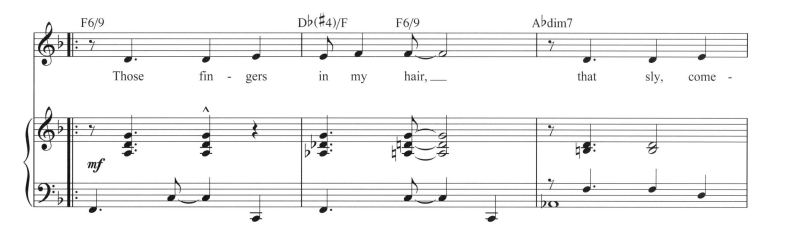

Those fin - gers in my hair, ___ that sly, come -

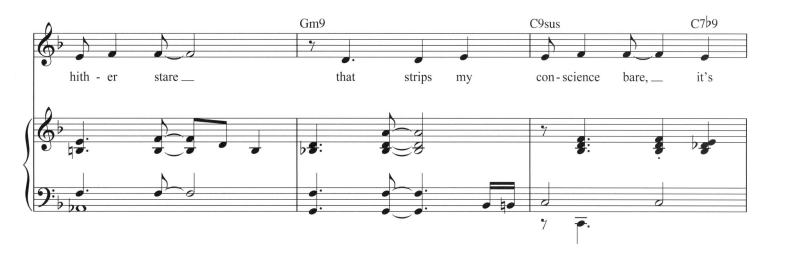

hith - er stare ___ that strips my con - science bare, ___ it's

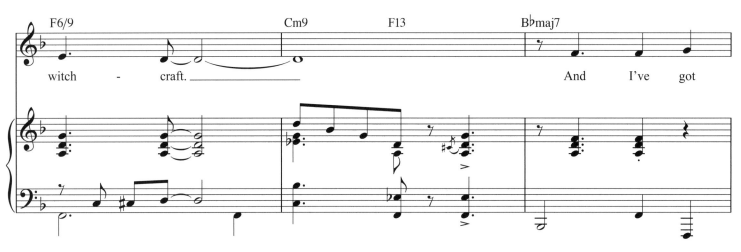

witch - craft. _____ And I've got

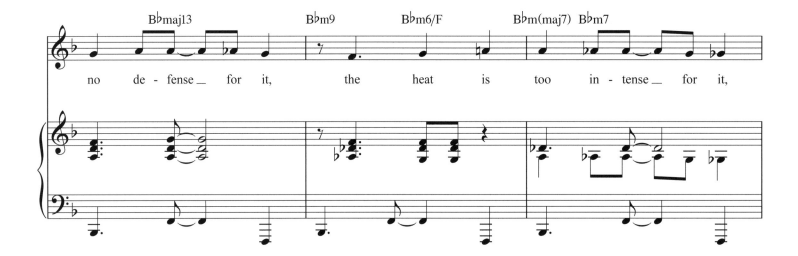

no de- fense ___ for it, the heat is too in- tense ___ for it,

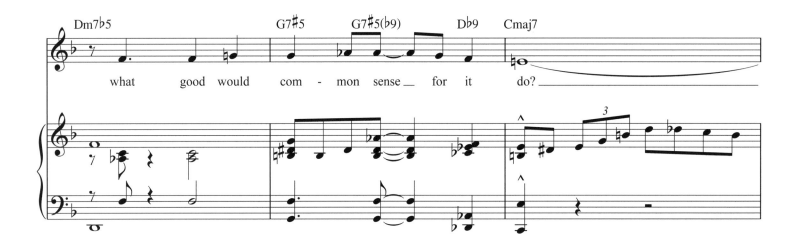

what good would com - mon sense ___ for it do? _____

___ 'Cause ___ it's witch - craft! ___ Wick - ed

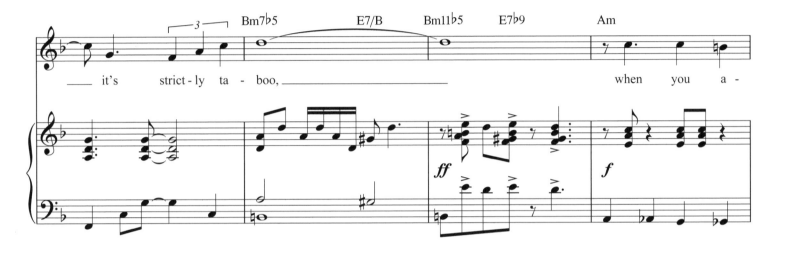

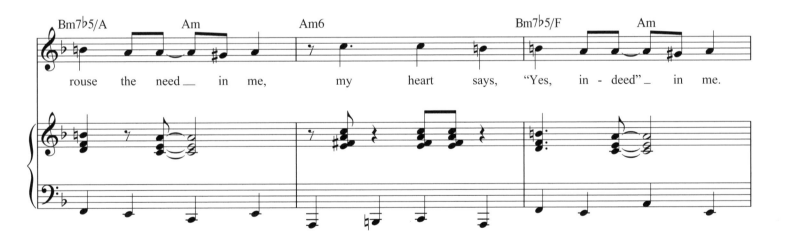

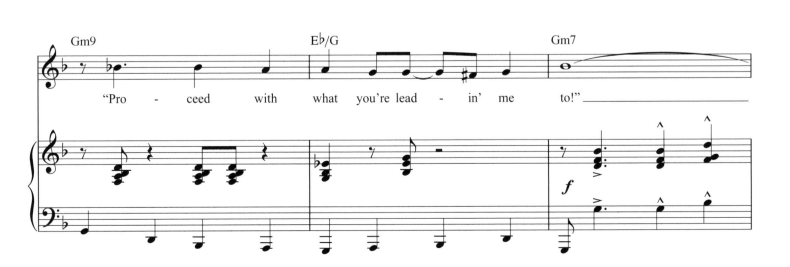

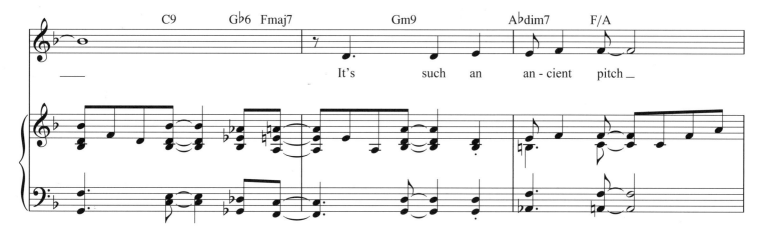

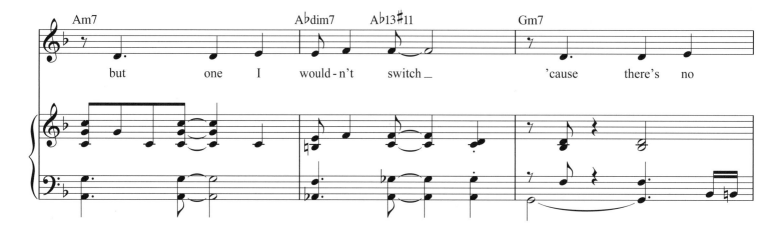

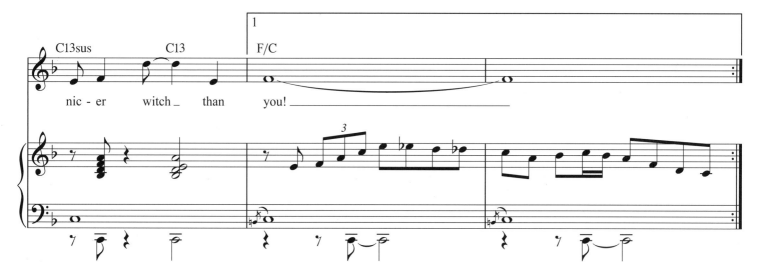

YESTERDAY

Words and Music by JOHN LENNON
and PAUL McCARTNEY

Jazz Ballad

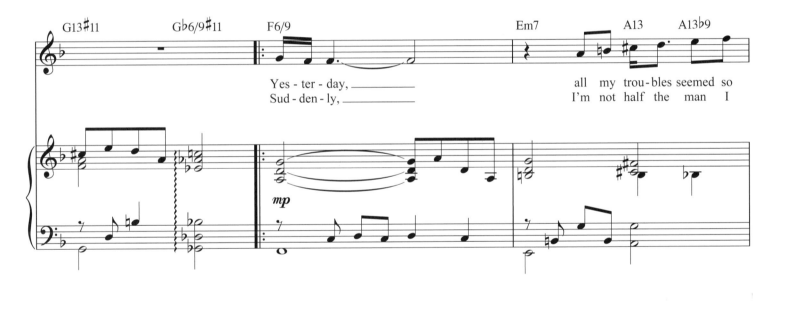

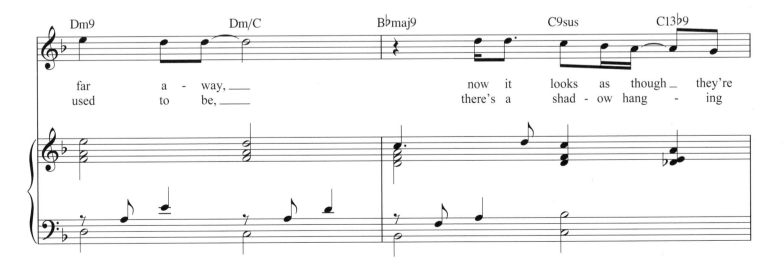

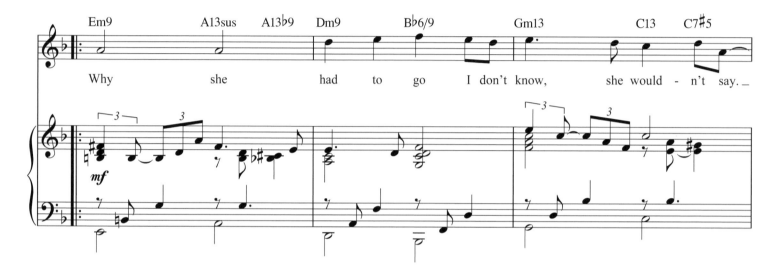

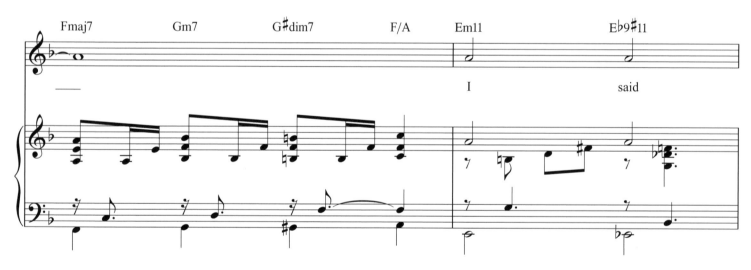

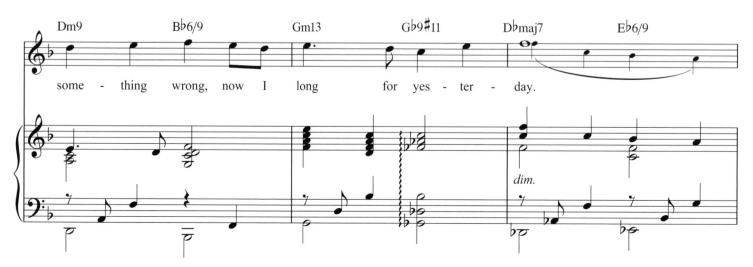

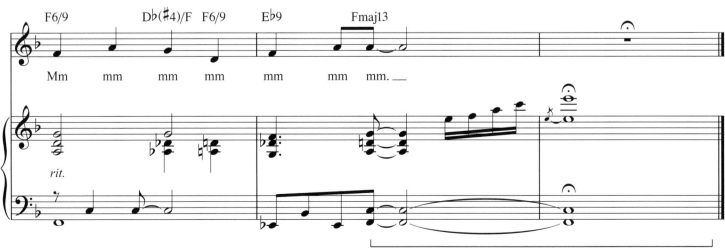

YOU ARE THE SUNSHINE OF MY LIFE

Words and Music by
STEVIE WONDER

Moderate Bossa Nova

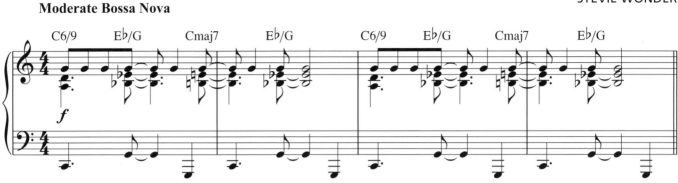

You are the sun - shine of __ my life, __

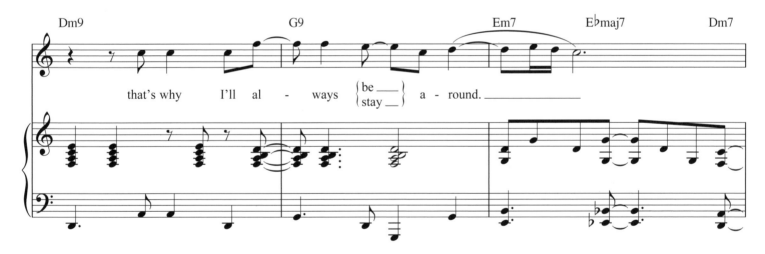

that's why I'll al - ways {be __ / stay __} a - round. __

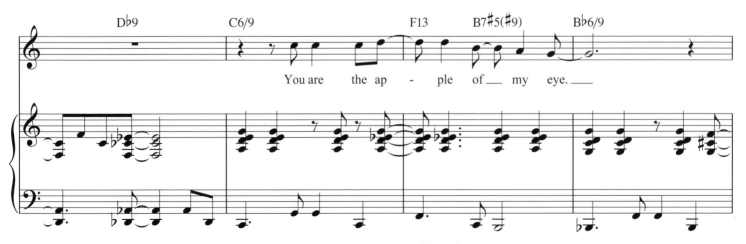

You are the ap - ple of __ my eye. __

For-ev - er you'll stay in my heart,

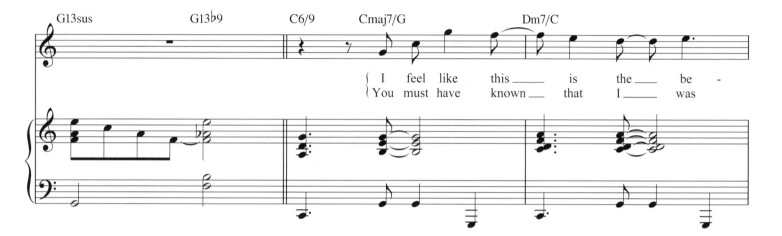

I feel like this is the be -
You must have known that I was

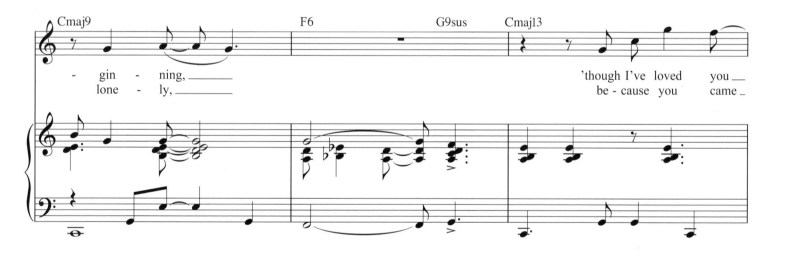

- gin - ning,
lone - ly,

'though I've loved you
be - cause you came

for a mil - lion years.
to my res - cue.

And if I thought
And I know that

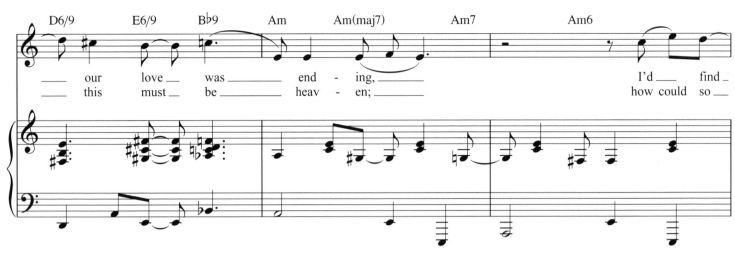

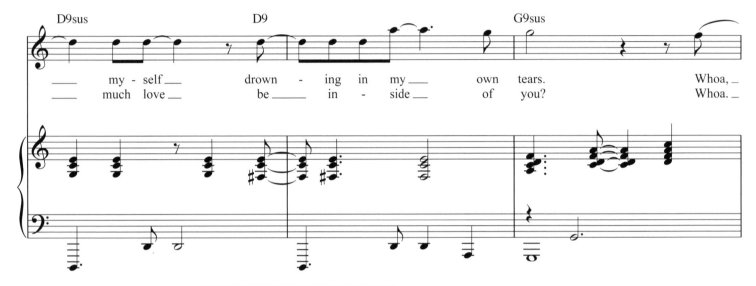

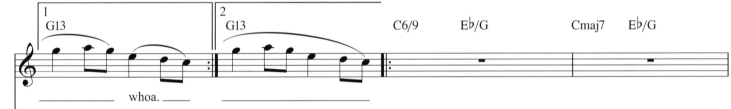

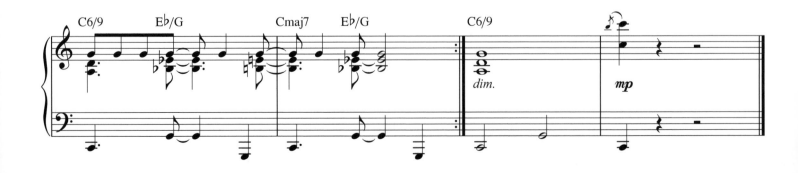